B♭ TENOR SAXOPHONE BOOK 3

ESSENTIAL TECHNIQUE for Band

INTERMEDIATE TO ADVANCED STUDIES

TIM LAUTZENHEISER • JOHN HIGGINS • CHARLES MENGHINI
PAUL LAVENDER • TOM C. RHODES • DON BIERSCHENK

To create an account, visit:
www.essentialelementsinteractive.com

Student Activation Code
E3TS-2346-8714-4089

ISBN 979-835013698-2

C MAJOR (Concert B♭ Major)

1. SCALE AND ARPEGGIO *Practice both upper and lower octaves.*

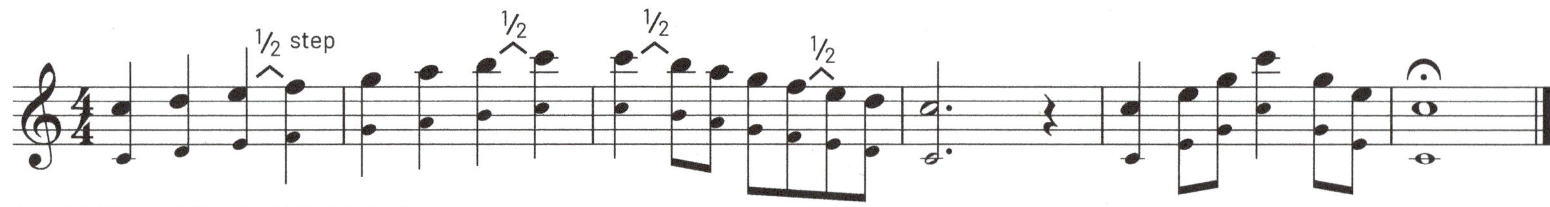

2. EXERCISE IN THIRDS

3. ARPEGGIO STUDY

4. TWO-PART ETUDE

5. CHROMATIC SCALE

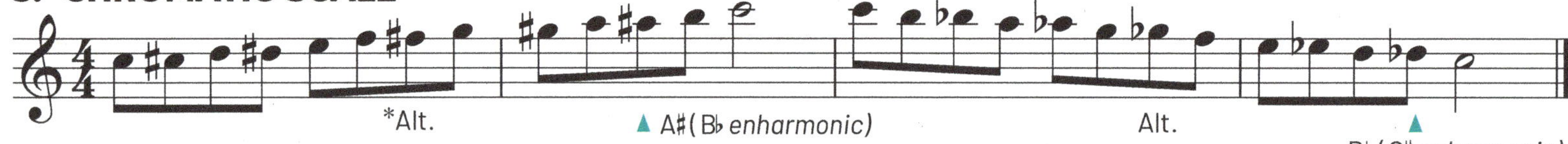

6. BALANCE BUILDER

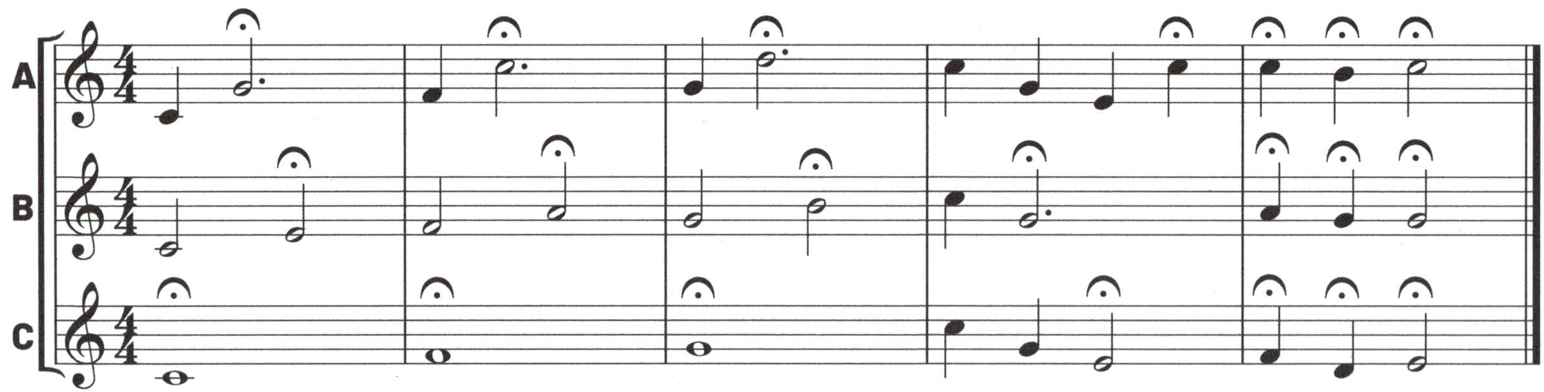

THEORY

divisi or *div.*	Divide the written parts among players, usually into two parts, with equal numbers playing each part.
unison or *a2*	All players play the same part (usually found after a *divisi* section).

7. CHORALE

*Remember to use Alternate F♯(G♭) whenever F♯ follows or precedes F♮.

8. GREAT GATE OF KIEV

Modeste Mussorgsky

E

Maestoso ◄ *Bold, stately*

f

▲ E

1.

2.

9. CHILDREN'S SHOES

African American Spiritual

Allegro

mf

1.

2.

HISTORY

English composer **George Frideric Handel** (1685–1759) is among the best known composers of the **Baroque Period (1600–1750)**. *Sound an Alarm* (from *Judas Maccabaeus*) and his most famous work, the *Hallelujah Chorus* (from *Messiah*), are two well-known melodies from his **oratorios** – large scale works for solo voices, chorus, and orchestra.

10. SOUND AN ALARM

George Frideric Handel

Allegro

f

mf

cresc.

f

11. HALLELUJAH CHORUS

George Frideric Handel

12. RHYTHM RAP *Clap the rhythm while counting and tapping.*

THEORY

3/8 Time Signature

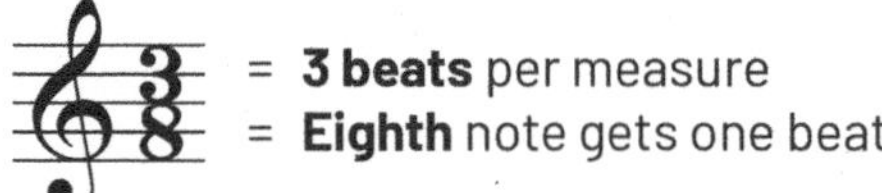

= **3 beats** per measure
= **Eighth** note gets one beat

♪ = 1 beat ♩ = 2 beats ♩. = 3 beats

3/8 time is usually played with a slight emphasis on the 1st beat of each measure. In faster music, this primary beat will make the music feel like it's counted "in 1."

13. RHYTHM RAP *Compare this exercise with No. 12.*

14. WALTZ PETITE

15. MOLLY BANN

English Folk Song

THEORY

9/8 Time Signature

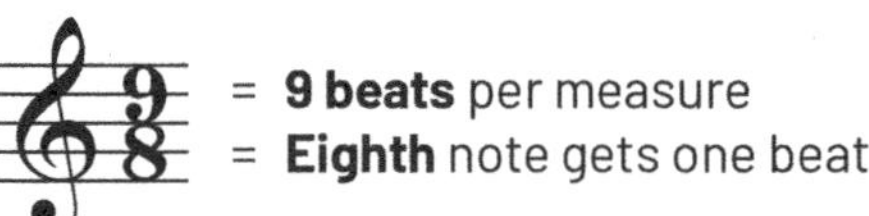

= **9 beats** per measure
= **Eighth** note gets one beat

♪ = 1 beat ♩. = 3 beats
♩ = 2 beats 𝅗𝅥. = 6 beats

9/8 time is usually played with a slight emphasis on the **1st**, **4th**, and **7th** beats of each measure. This divides the measure into 3 groups of 3 beats each. In faster music, these three primary beats will make the music feel like it's counted "in 3."

16. RHYTHM RAP *Clap the rhythm while counting and tapping.*

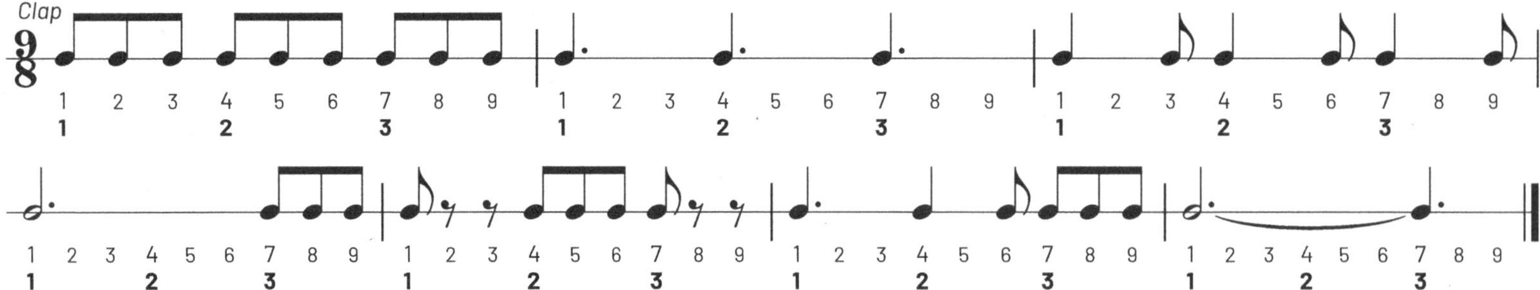

17. SUNDAY AT NINE

A MINOR (Concert G Minor)

Minor Keys

Minor keys and their scales sound different from major keys because of their different pattern of whole and half steps. Each minor key is *relative* or "related" to the major key with the same key signature.

The simplest form of a minor key is called **natural minor**. Two other types are **harmonic minor** and **melodic minor**, each of which have certain altered tones.

18. NATURAL MINOR

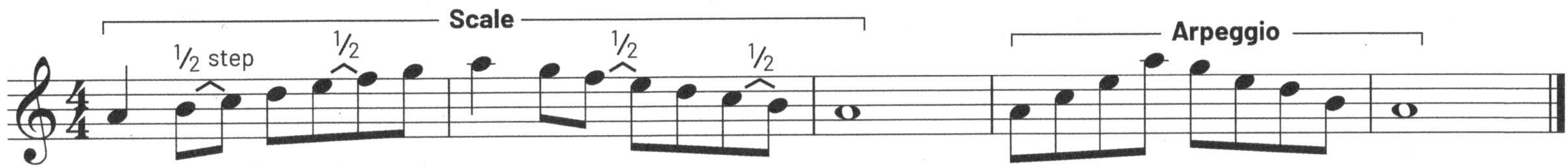

19. HARMONIC MINOR

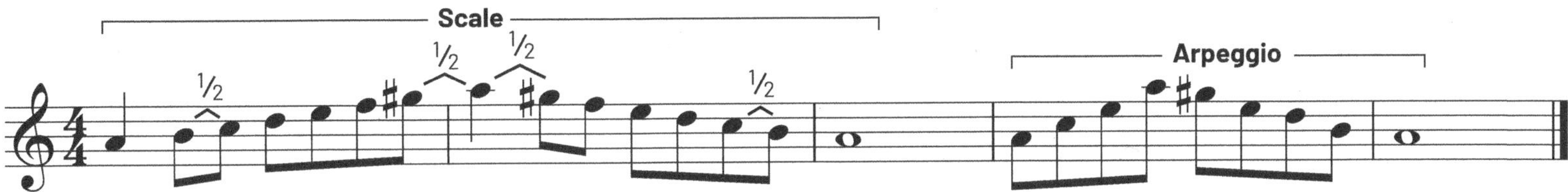

20. PAT-A-PAN

French

21. THE SLEDGEHAMMER SONG

Russian

22. ESSENTIAL ELEMENTS QUIZ – AUSTRALIAN FOLK SONG

Australian

F MAJOR (Concert E♭ Major)

23. SCALE AND ARPEGGIO *Practice both upper and lower octaves.*

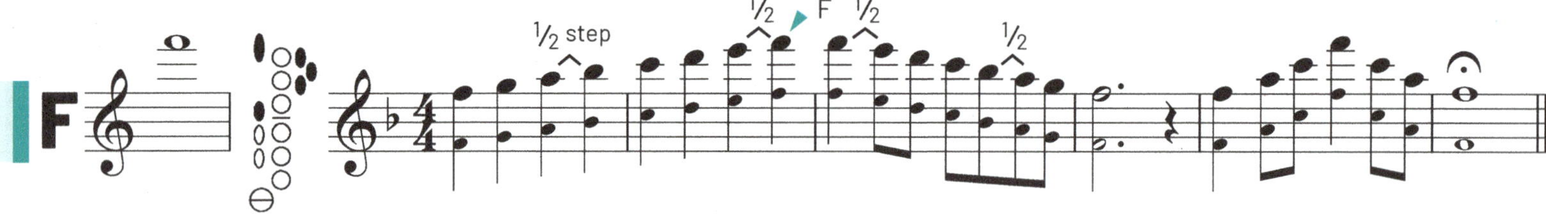

24. EXERCISE IN THIRDS

25. ARPEGGIO STUDY

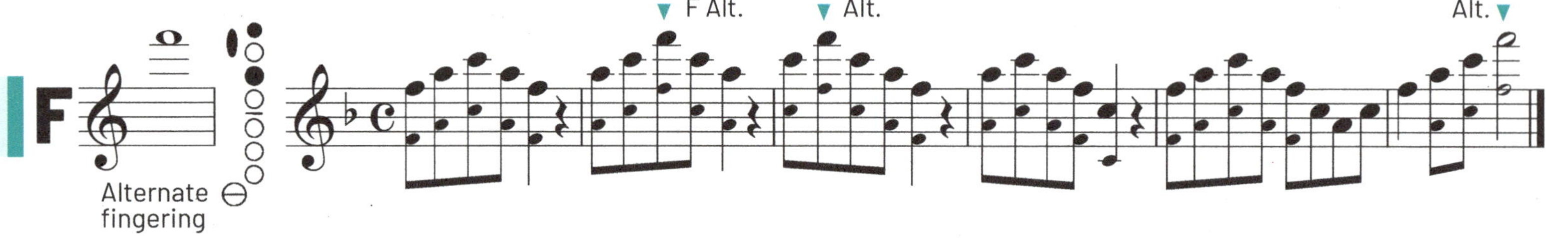

26. TWO-PART ETUDE

27. CHROMATIC SCALE

28. BALANCE BUILDER

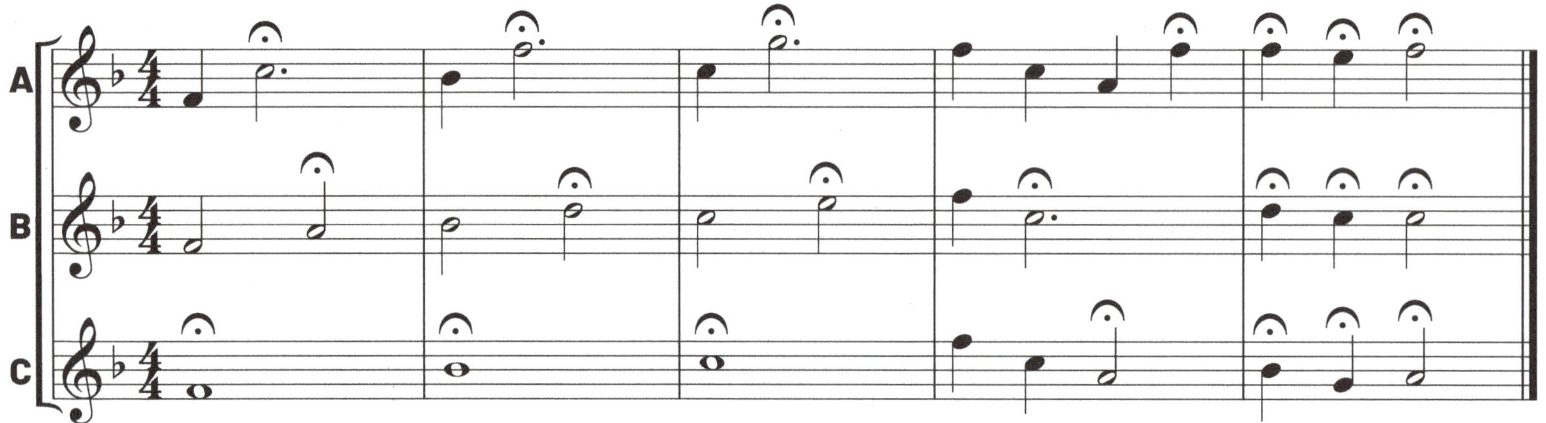

29. CHORALE

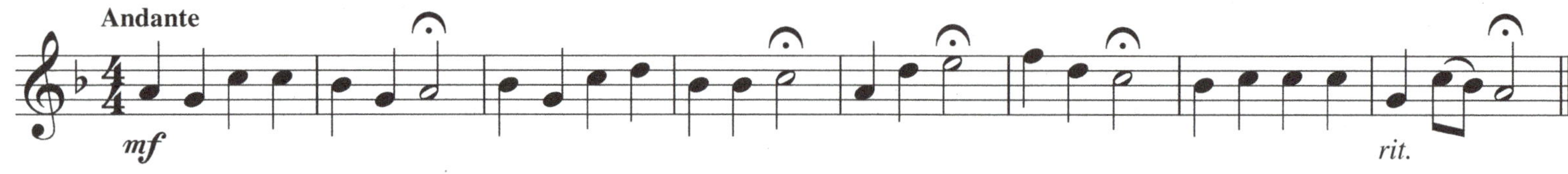

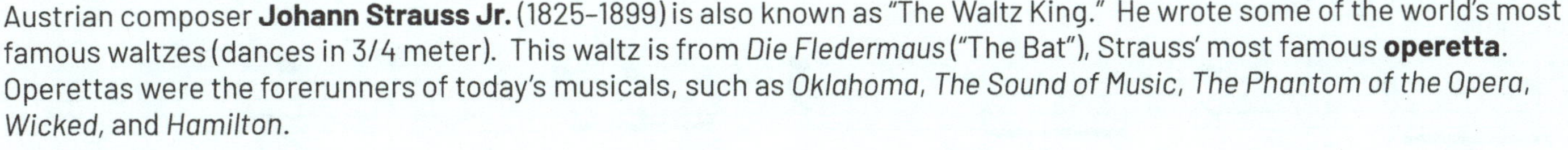
Austrian composer **Johann Strauss Jr.** (1825–1899) is also known as "The Waltz King." He wrote some of the world's most famous waltzes (dances in 3/4 meter). This waltz is from *Die Fledermaus* ("The Bat"), Strauss' most famous **operetta**. Operettas were the forerunners of today's musicals, such as *Oklahoma*, *The Sound of Music*, *The Phantom of the Opera*, *Wicked*, and *Hamilton*.

HISTORY

30. ADELE'S SONG

Johann Strauss Jr.

Tempo di valse ◄ *Waltz tempo*

f *p* *mf* 1. 2. *f*

31. MARINE'S HYMN

Allegro

f 1. 2.

32. RHYTHM RAP

Clap

Count 1 & 2 e & a 1 & 2 & 1 & 2 e & a 1 & 2 & 1 & 2 e & a 1 & 2 & 1 & 2 e & a 1 & 2 &

Tap ↓ ↑ ↓ ↑ ↓ ↑ ↓ ↑ ↓ ↑ ↓ ↑ ↓ ↑ ↓ ↑ ↓ ↑ ↓ ↑ ↓ ↑ ↓ ↑ ↓ ↑ ↓ ↑ ↓ ↑ ↓ ↑

33. KEEPIN' SECRETS

Appalachian Folk Song

Moderato

mf

34. THE KEEL ROW

Sea Song

Moderato

mf

▲ *Count carefully!*

35. JACK'S THE MAN

THEORY

12/8 Time Signature

♪ = 1 beat ♩. = 3 beats 𝅗𝅥.‿♩. = 9 beats
♩ = 2 beats 𝅗𝅥. = 6 beats 𝅝. = 12 beats

12/8 time is usually played with a slight emphasis on the **1st**, **4th**, **7th** and **10th** beats of each measure. This divides the measure into 4 groups of 3 beats each. These four primary beats will make the music feel like it's counted "in 4."

36. RHYTHM RAP *Clap the rhythm while counting and tapping.*

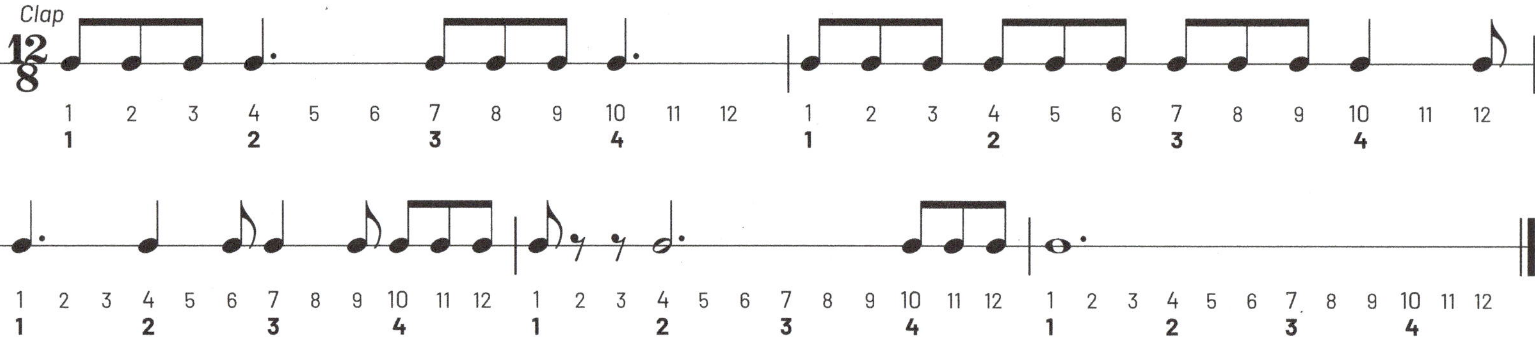

37. SERENADE

38. WITH THINE EYES

D MINOR (Concert C Minor)

39. NATURAL MINOR *Practice both upper and lower octaves.*

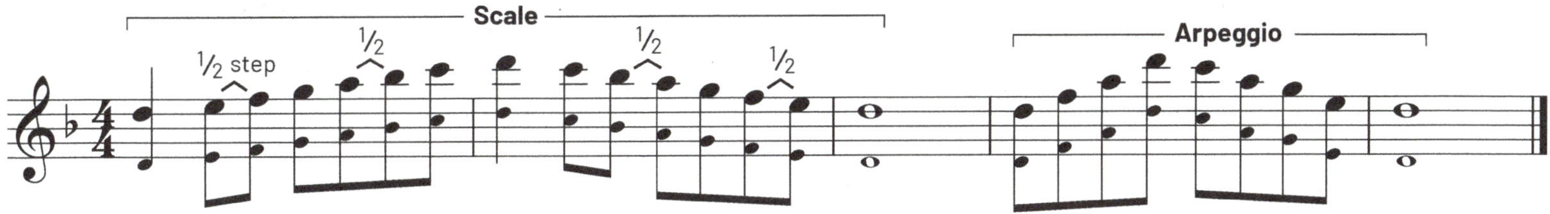

40. HARMONIC MINOR

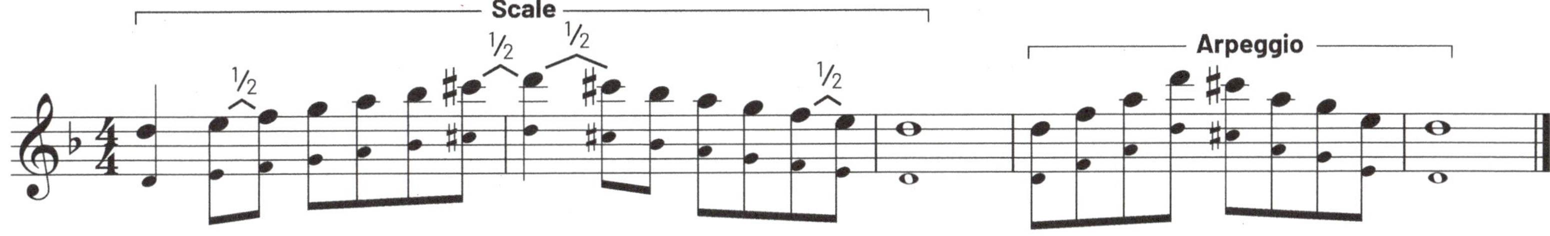

HISTORY

Even today, **Native American Indian music** continues to be an important part of tribal dancing ceremonies, using Apache fiddles, rattles, flutes, and log drums to accompany simple songs. American composer **Charles Wakefield Cadman** (1881–1946) wrote this song in 1914 based on Indian melodies he researched throughout his lifetime.

41. SONG OF THE WEEPING SPIRIT

Native American Indian Melody
Adapt. Charles Wakefield Cadman

Lento mysterioso ◄ *Slowly and mysteriously*

42. SCOTTISH LEGEND

Amy Marcy Beach

43. ESSENTIAL ELEMENTS QUIZ *Which measures sound major and which ones minor?*

G MAJOR (Concert F Major)

44. SCALE AND ARPEGGIO

45. EXERCISE IN THIRDS

46. ARPEGGIO STUDY

47. TWO-PART ETUDE

48. CHROMATIC SCALE

49. BALANCE BUILDER

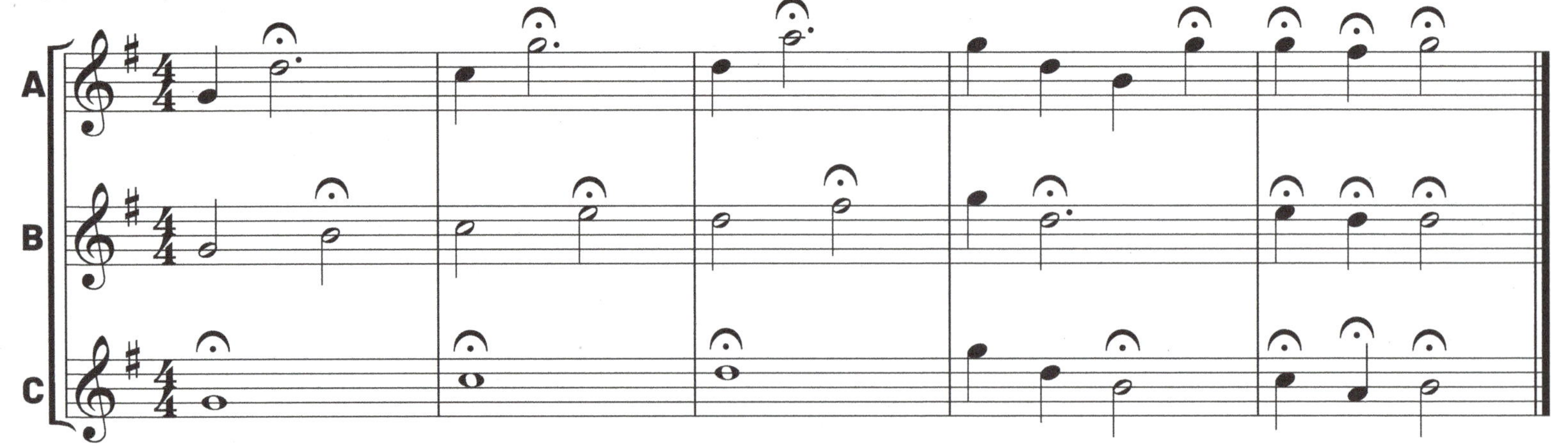

50. CHORALE

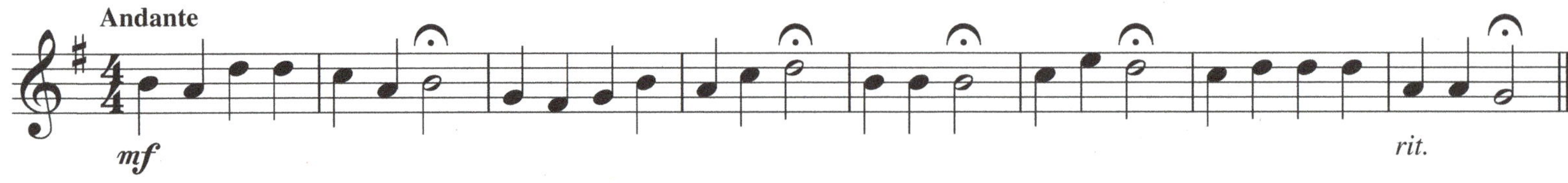

51. REST ALERT

52. RHYTHM RAP

53. ISLAND SONG

French composer **Claude Debussy** (1862–1918) created moods and "impressions" with his music. While earlier composers used music to describe events (such as Tchaikovsky's *1812 Overture*), Debussy's new ideas helped shape today's music. The style of art and music created in this time is called "impressionism." The first automobile was produced during Debussy's lifetime. He died the same year that World War I ended.

54. THE LITTLE CHILD

Claude Debussy

Triplets with Rests

Triplets that start or end with a rest are usually marked with a bracket ⌐3¬

THEORY

55. TRIPLET AND REST VARIATIONS

56. TURKEY IN THE STRAW

American Folk Song

57. ESSENTIAL ELEMENTS QUIZ

Write the first 2 lines of exercise 56 in cut time.

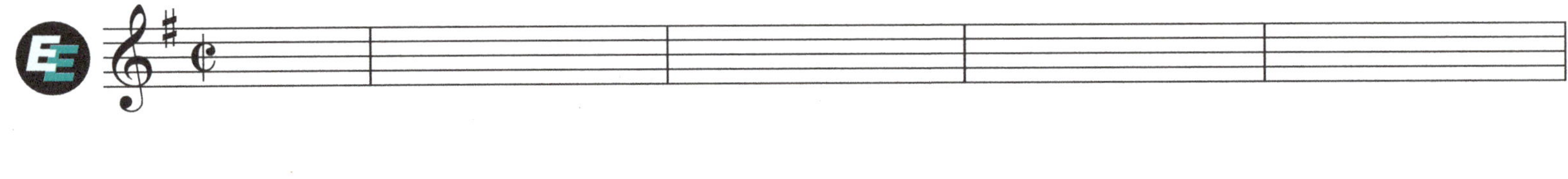

THEORY

Sixteenth Notes and Rests in $\frac{6}{8}$, $\frac{3}{8}$, $\frac{9}{8}$, $\frac{12}{8}$

♬ = ½ beat 𝅀 = ½ beat ♩ = 2 beats 𝄽 = 2 beats

♪ = 1 beat 𝄾 = 1 beat ♩. = 3 beats 𝄽. = 3 beats

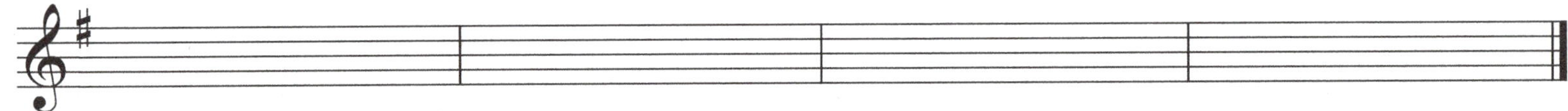

58. RHYTHM RAP

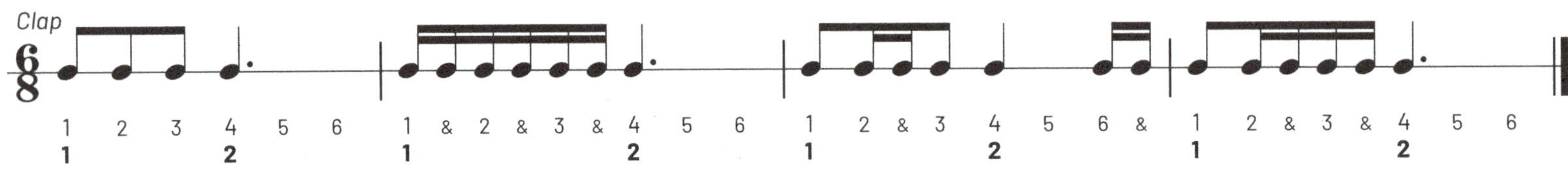

59. SONATINA

E MINOR (Concert D Minor)

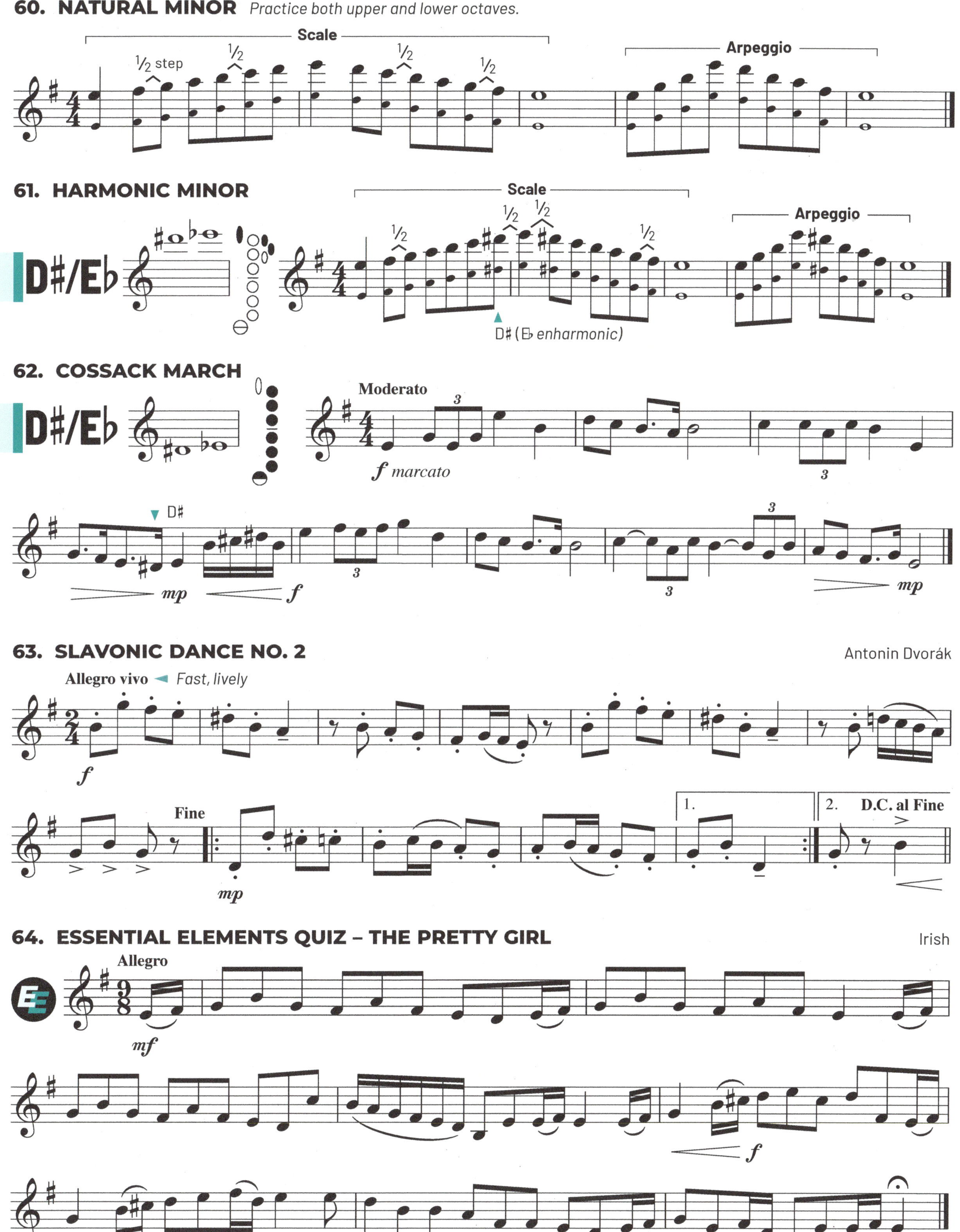

B♭ MAJOR (Concert A♭ Major)

65. SCALE AND ARPEGGIO *Practice both upper and lower octaves.*

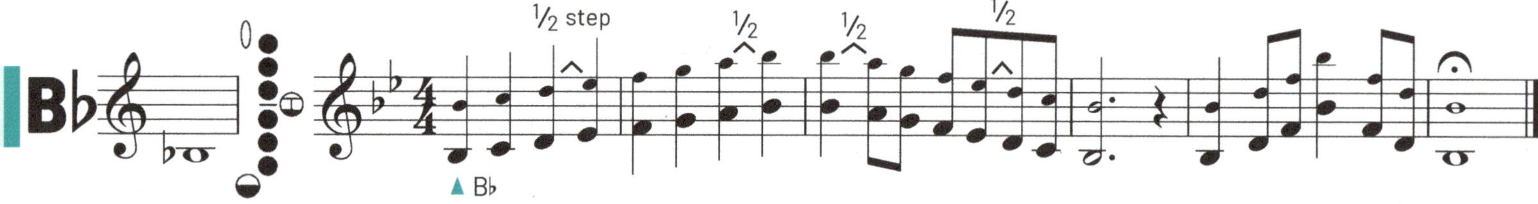

66. EXERCISE IN THIRDS

67. ARPEGGIO STUDY

68. TWO-PART ETUDE

69. CHROMATIC SCALE

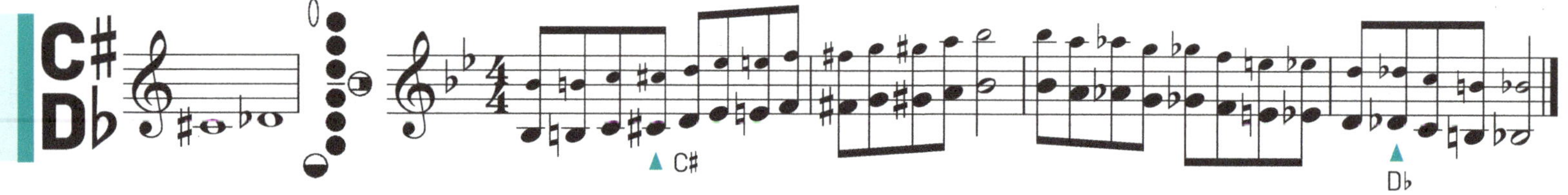

70. BALANCE BUILDER

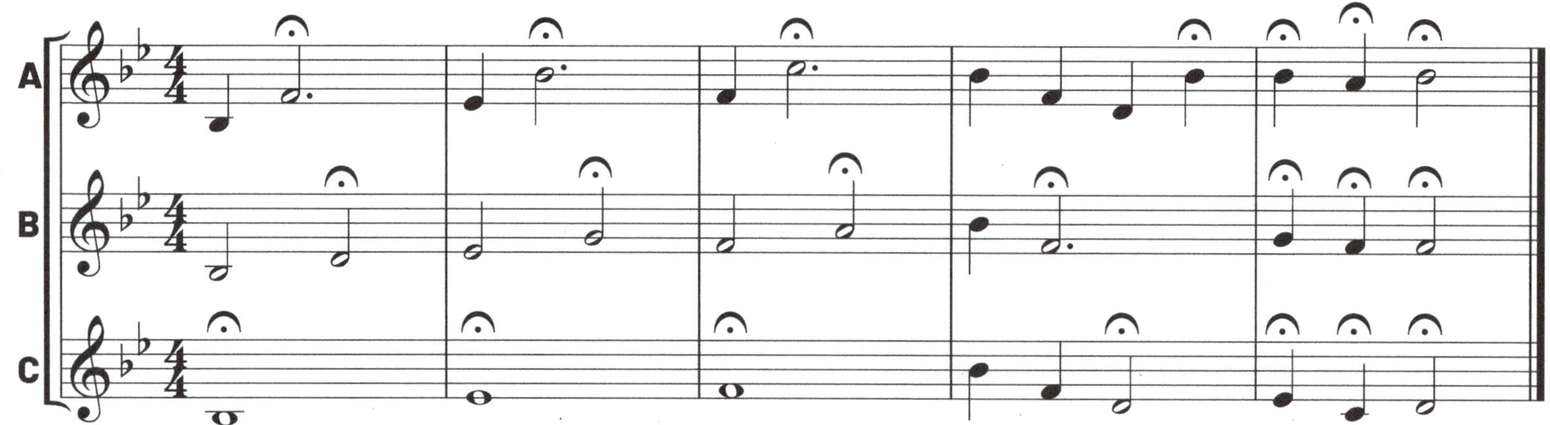

71. CHORALE

*Forked B♭ (F) is convenient to use in a B♭ major arpeggio.

The Star Spangled Banner is the national anthem of the United States of America. Francis Scott Key wrote the words during the 1814 battle at Fort McHenry. He listened to the sounds of the fighting throughout the night while being detained on a ship. At dawn, he saw the American flag still flying over the fort. He was inspired to write these words, which were later set to the melody of a popular English song.

HISTORY

72. THE STAR SPANGLED BANNER

Words by Francis Scott Key
Music by John Stafford Smith

Allegro maestoso

f Oh— say can you see, by the dawn's ear - ly light, what so proud - ly we

hailed at the twi - light's last gleam - ing? Whose broad stripes and bright stars, through the

per - il - ous fight, o'er the ram - parts we watched were so gal - lant - ly

stream - ing. And the rock - et's red glare, the bombs burst - ing in air, gave
mf

proof through the night that our flag was still there. Oh say does that— Star Span - gled
f

Ban - ner— yet— wave— o'er the land— of the free and the home of the brave?

Dynamics

pp – *pianissimo* (play very softly) ***ff*** – *fortissimo* (play very loudly)
Remember to use full breath support to produce the best possible tone and intonation.

THEORY

73. INTERMEZZO

74. RHYTHM RAP

75. MORNING STAR

76. SONATA

Wolfgang Amadeus Mozart

77. RONDEAU

Jean-Joseph Mouret

Grace Note A small note (or notes) which is played on, or slightly before the beat.

78. JULIET'S WALTZ

Charles Gounod

G MINOR (Concert F Minor)

79. NATURAL MINOR

80. HARMONIC MINOR

81. SORCERER'S APPRENTICE

82. I WALK THE ROAD AGAIN

American

83. ESSENTIAL ELEMENTS QUIZ – GREENSLEEVES

English Folk Song

D MAJOR (Concert C Major)

84. SCALE AND ARPEGGIO *Practice both upper and lower octaves.*

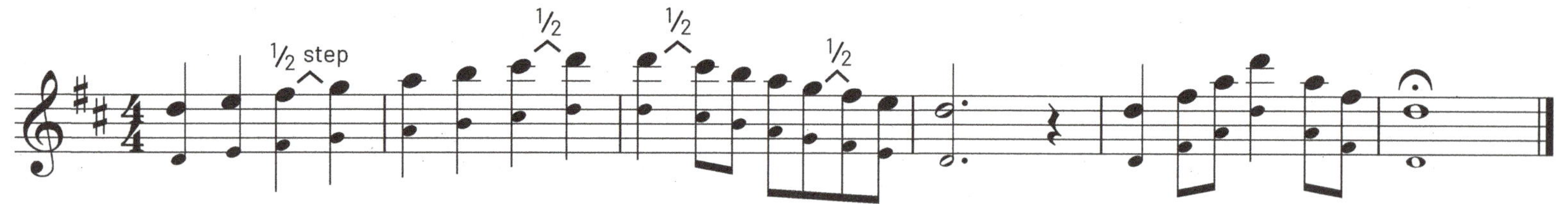

85. EXERCISE IN THIRDS

86. ARPEGGIO STUDY

87. TWO-PART ETUDE

88. CHROMATIC SCALE

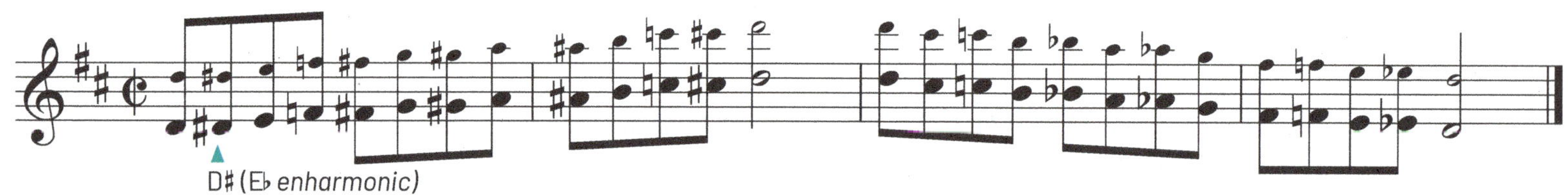

89. BALANCE BUILDER

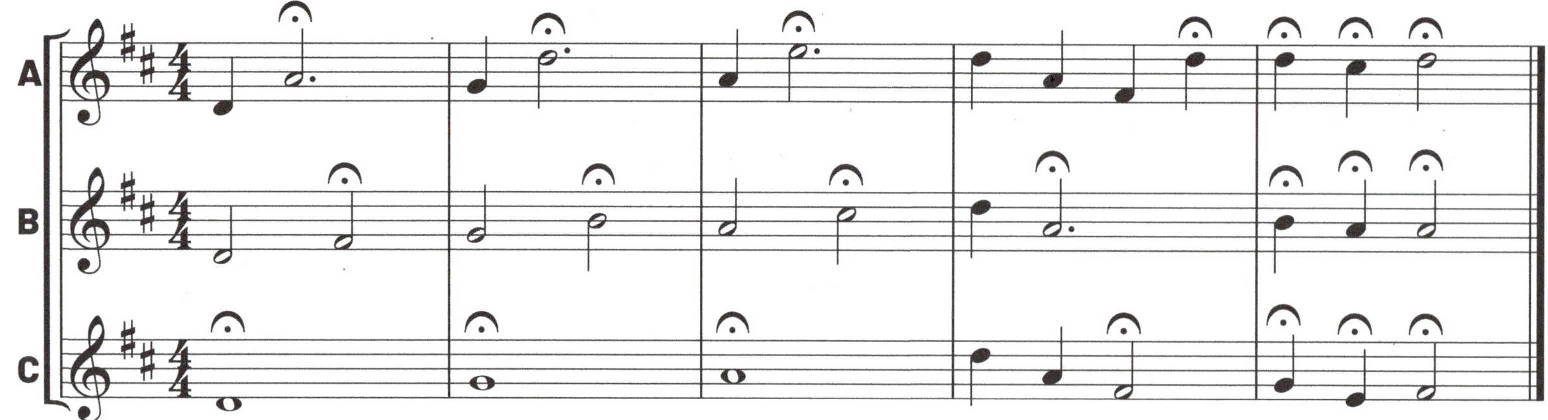

90. CHORALE

African American spirituals originated in the 1700's. As one of the largest categories of true American folk music, these melodies were sung and passed on for generations without being written down. Black and white people worked together to publish the first spiritual collection in 1867, four years after *The Emancipation Proclamation* was signed into law.

91. SIT DOWN, SISTER

African American Spiritual

THEORY

Quarter Note Triplets

Similar to eighth note triplets where 1 beat is divided into 3 equal notes,

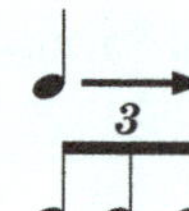

quarter note triplets divide 2 beats into 3 equal notes.

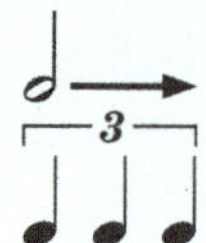

93. RHYTHM RAP

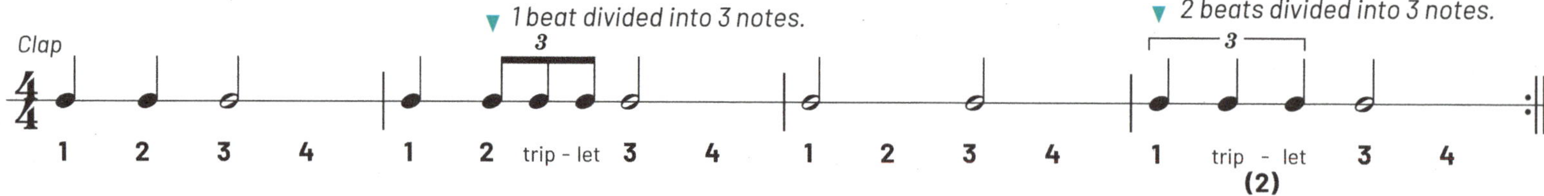

94. THREE FOR TWO

95. SURIRAM'S SONG

Malaysian Folk Song

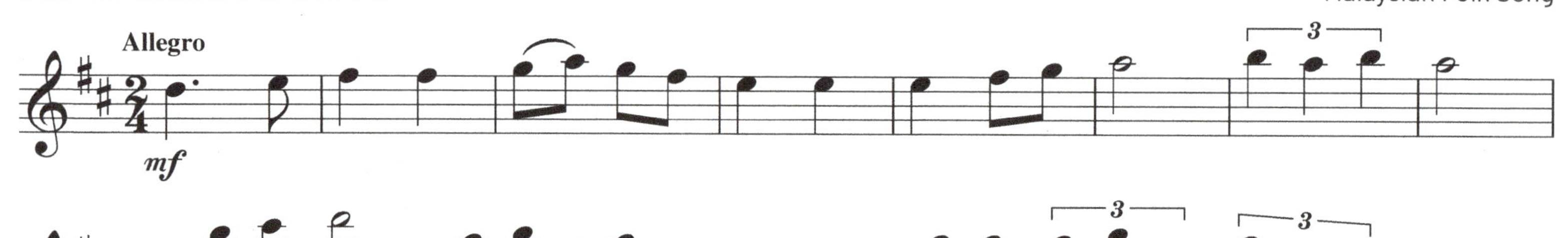

HISTORY

Africa is a large continent that is made up of many nations, and **African folk music** is as diverse as its many cultures. Folk songs from any country are expressions of work, love, war, sadness, and joy. This song is from Tanzania. The words describe a rabbit hopping and running through a field. Listen to the percussion section play African-sounding drums and rhythms.

96. JIBULI (The Rabbit's Song)

Adapted Tanzanian Folk Song

B MINOR (Concert A Minor)

97. NATURAL MINOR *Practice both upper and lower octaves.*

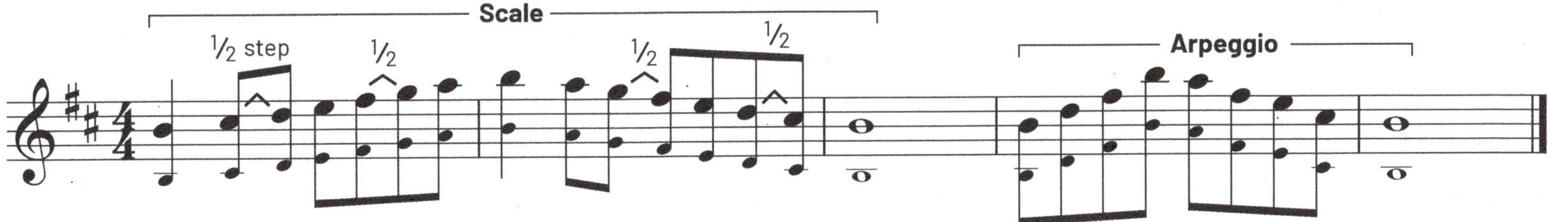

98. HARMONIC MINOR

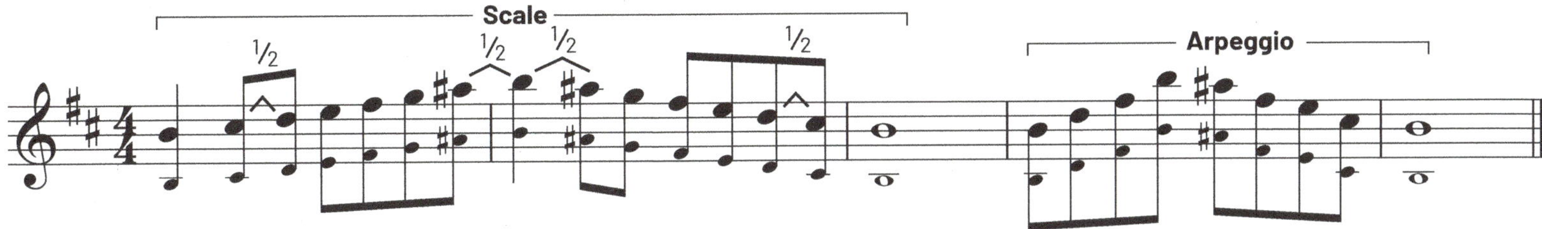

Meter Changes

THEORY

Meter changes, or changing time signatures within a section of music, are commonly found in contemporary music. Composers use this technique to create a unique rhythm, pulse, or musical style.

99. TIME ZONES

HISTORY

Important French composers of the late 19th century include **Claude Debussy** (1862–1918), **Gabriel Fauré** (1845–1924), **Erik Satie** (1866–1925), **César Franck** (1822–1890), **Camille Saint-Saëns** (1835–1921), and **Paul Dukas** (1865–1935). Their works continue to have influence on the music of modern day composers. Gabriel Fauré wrote *Pavanne* (originally for orchestra) in 1887, two years before the Eiffel Tower was completed in Paris.

100. PAVANNE

Gabriel Fauré

E♭ MAJOR (Concert D♭ Major)

101. SCALE AND ARPEGGIO *Practice both upper and lower octaves.*

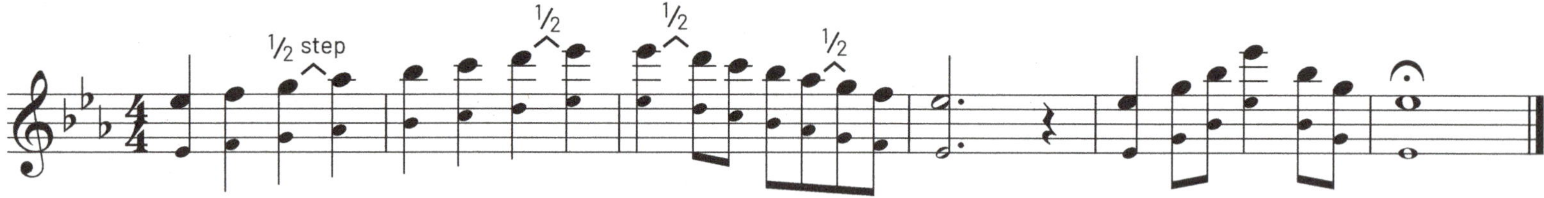

102. EXERCISE IN THIRDS

103. ARPEGGIO STUDY

104. TWO-PART ETUDE

105. CHROMATIC SCALE

106. BALANCE BUILDER

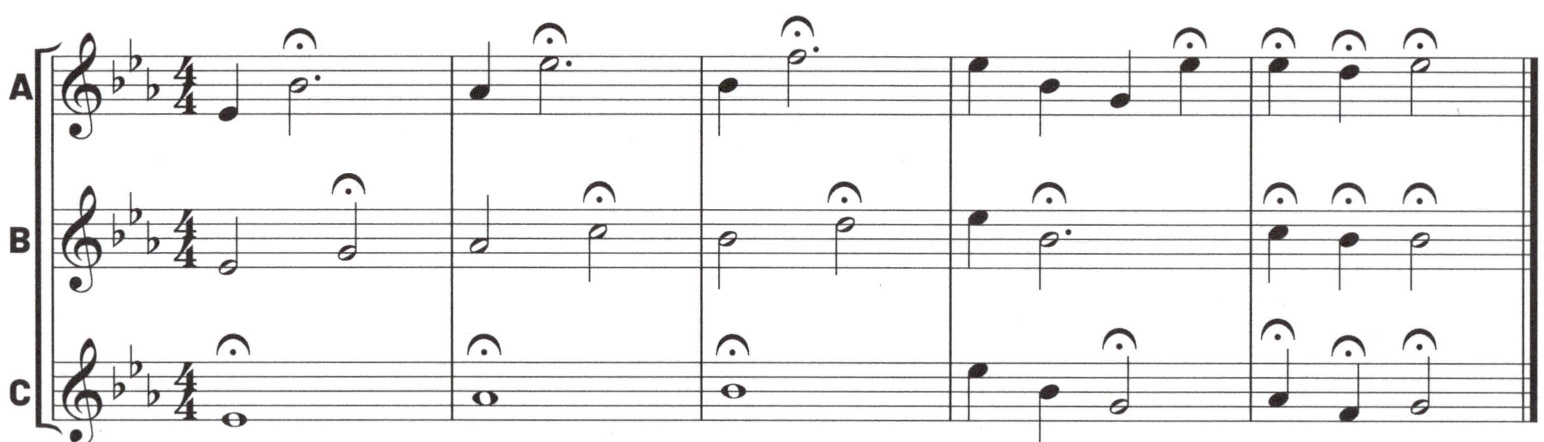

107. CHORALE

108. GERMAN NATIONAL ANTHEM
Franz Josef Haydn
Maestoso
mf
f
109. JOY
Johann Sebastian Bach
Andante espressivo ◄ Expressively
mp
rit.
5/4 Time Signature
= 5 beats per measure
= Quarter note gets one beat
Conducting
Practice conducting these five-beat patterns.
or
THEORY
110. RHYTHM RAP
Clap
1 2 & 3 4 5 1 2 3 4 5
111. LET'S COUNT FIVE
Moderato
mf
sfz

112. SUKURU ITO

African Folk Song

HISTORY

English composer **George Frideric Handel** (1685–1759) lived during the **Baroque Period (1600–1750)**. *Water Music* was written in honor of England's King George I. The first performance took place on the Thames River on July 17, 1717. Fifty musicians performed the work while floating on a barge. Handel lived during the same time as Johann Sebastian Bach, perhaps the most famous Baroque composer.

113. WATER MUSIC

George Frideric Handel

114. ESSENTIAL TECHNIQUE QUIZ – PICTURES AT AN EXHIBITION

Modeste Mussorgsky

C MINOR (Concert B♭ Minor)

115. NATURAL MINOR *Practice both upper and lower octaves.*

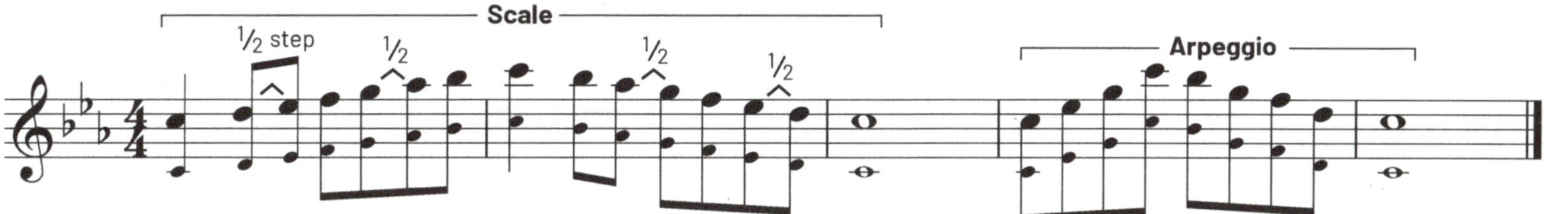

116. HARMONIC MINOR

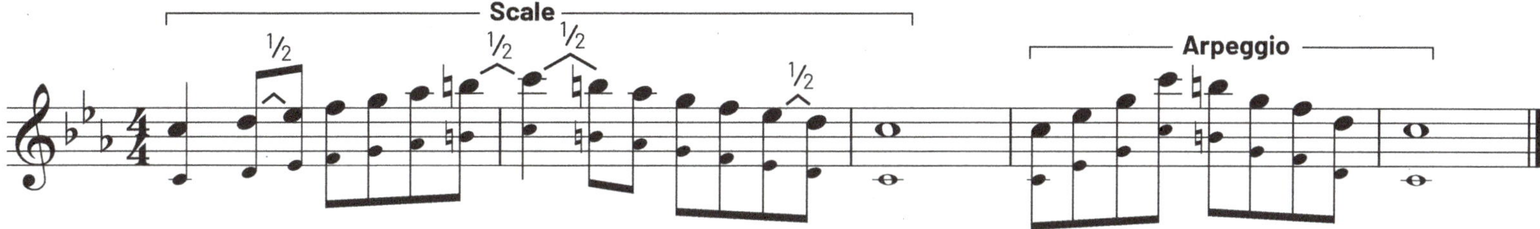

Ostinato A clear and distinct musical phrase that is repeated persistently.

THEORY

British composer **Gustav Holst** (1874–1934) is one of the most widely played composers for concert band today. Many of his compositions, including his familiar military suites, are based on tuneful English folk songs. His most famous work for orchestra, *The Planets* (1916), has seven movements—one written for each known planet, excluding Earth.

HISTORY

117. MARS – Duet/Trio

Gustav Holst

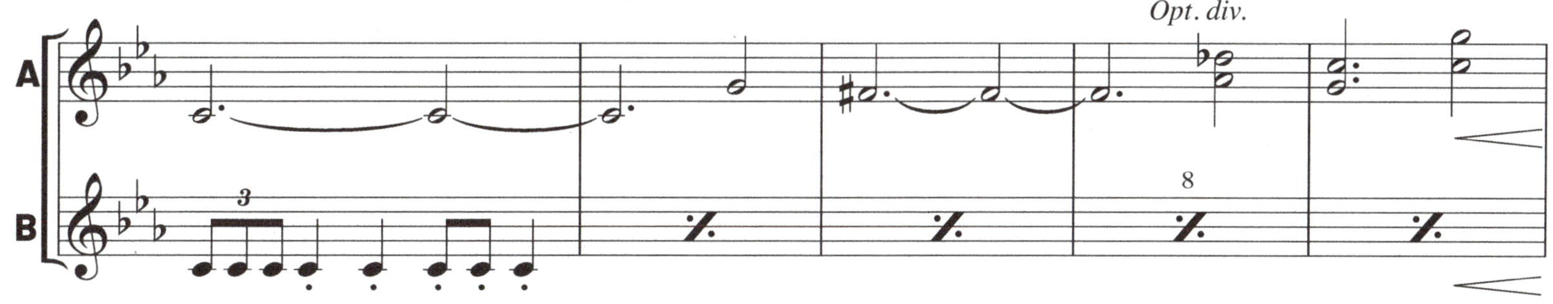

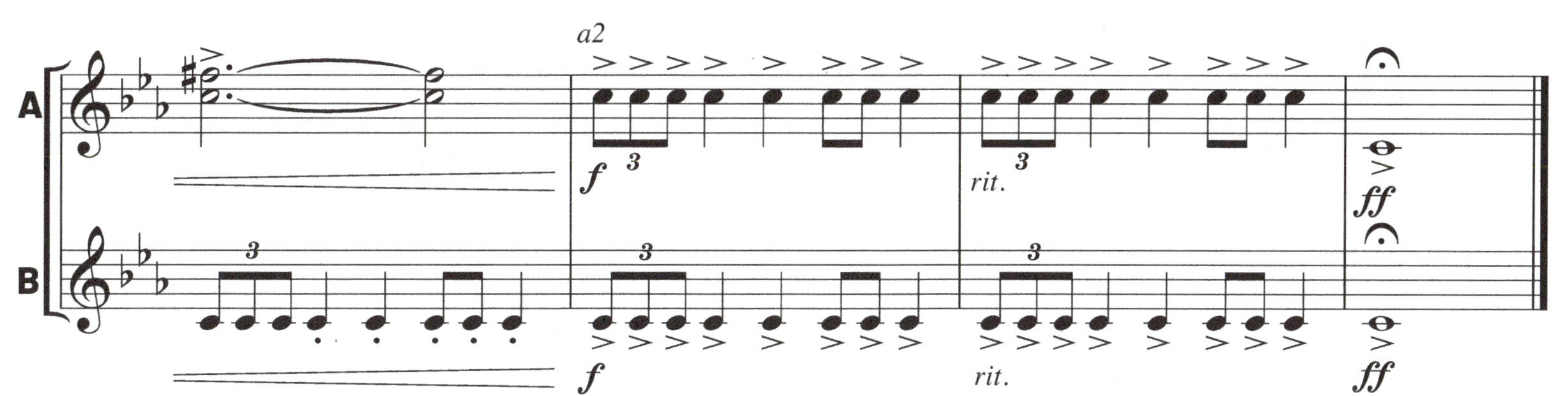

A MAJOR (Concert G Major)

118. SCALE AND ARPEGGIO

119. EXERCISE IN THIRDS

120. ARPEGGIO STUDY

121. TWO-PART ETUDE

122. CHROMATIC SCALE

123. BALANCE BUILDER

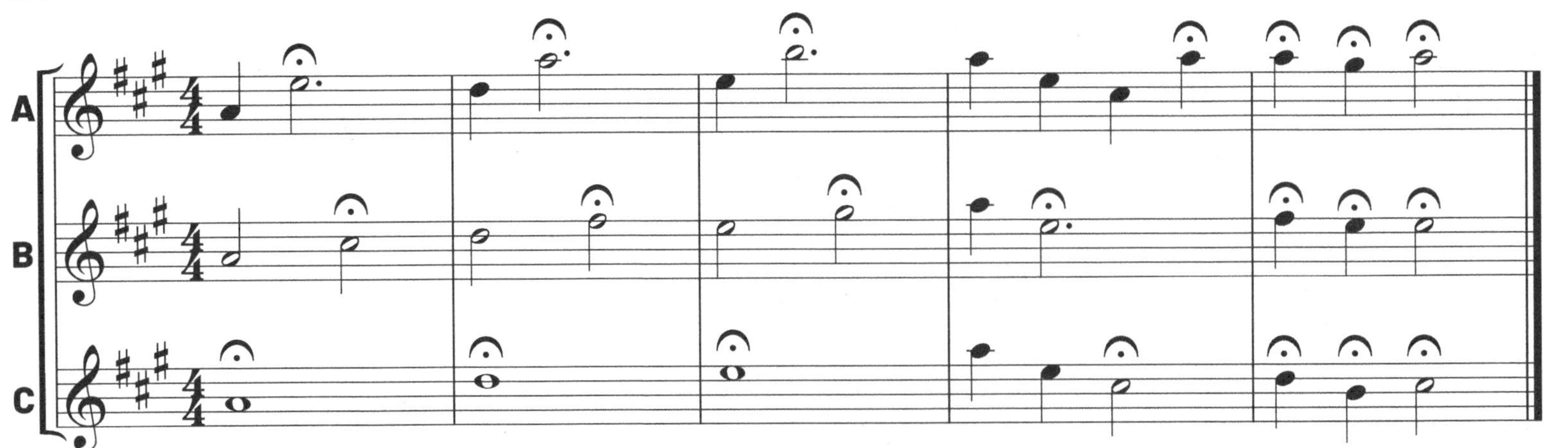

124. CHORALE

Norwegian composer **Edvard Grieg** (1843–1907) based much of his music on the folk songs and dances of Norway. During the late 19th century, composers often used melodies from their native land. This trend is called **nationalism**. Russian **Modeste Mussorgsky** (1839–1881), Czech **Antonin Dvořák** (1841–1904), and Englishman **Sir Edward Elgar** (1857–1934) are other famous composers whose music was influenced by nationalism.

HISTORY

125. NORWEGIAN DANCE

Edvard Grieg

126. FRENCH NATIONAL ANTHEM (LA MARSEILLAISE)

Rouget De L'Isle

Music written during the **Renaissance Period (1430–1600)** was often upbeat and dance-like. *Wolsey's Wilde* was originally written for the lute, an ancestor to the guitar and the most popular instrument of the Renaissance era. Modern day concert band composer Gordon Jacob used this popular song in his *William Byrd Suite*, written as a tribute to English composer William Byrd (1543–1623).

HISTORY

127. WOLSEY'S WILDE

Anonymous

Animato ◄ *Animated, lively*

F♯ MINOR (Concert E Minor)

128. NATURAL MINOR

129. HARMONIC MINOR

Scale

½ ½ ½ ½

Arpeggio

▲ E♯ (F♮ *enharmonic*)

HISTORY

Native Japanese instruments include the *shakuhachi*, a bamboo flute played pointing downward; the *koto*, a long zither with movable frets played sitting down; and the *gakubiwa*, a pear-shaped lute with strings that are plucked. These instruments have been an important part of Japanese culture since the 8th century. *Kabuki*, a Japanese theatrical form that originated in 1603, remains popular in Japan. Performers play native Japanese instruments during Kabuki performances.

130. SONG OF THE SHAKUHACHI

Japanese Folk Song

THEORY

D.C. al Coda At the **D.C. al Coda**, play again from the beginning to the indication **To Coda** ⊕, then skip to the section marked ⊕ **Coda**, meaning "ending section."

D.S. al Coda Similar to **D.C. al Coda**, but return to the sign 𝄋.

131. POLOVETZIAN DANCES

Alexander Borodin

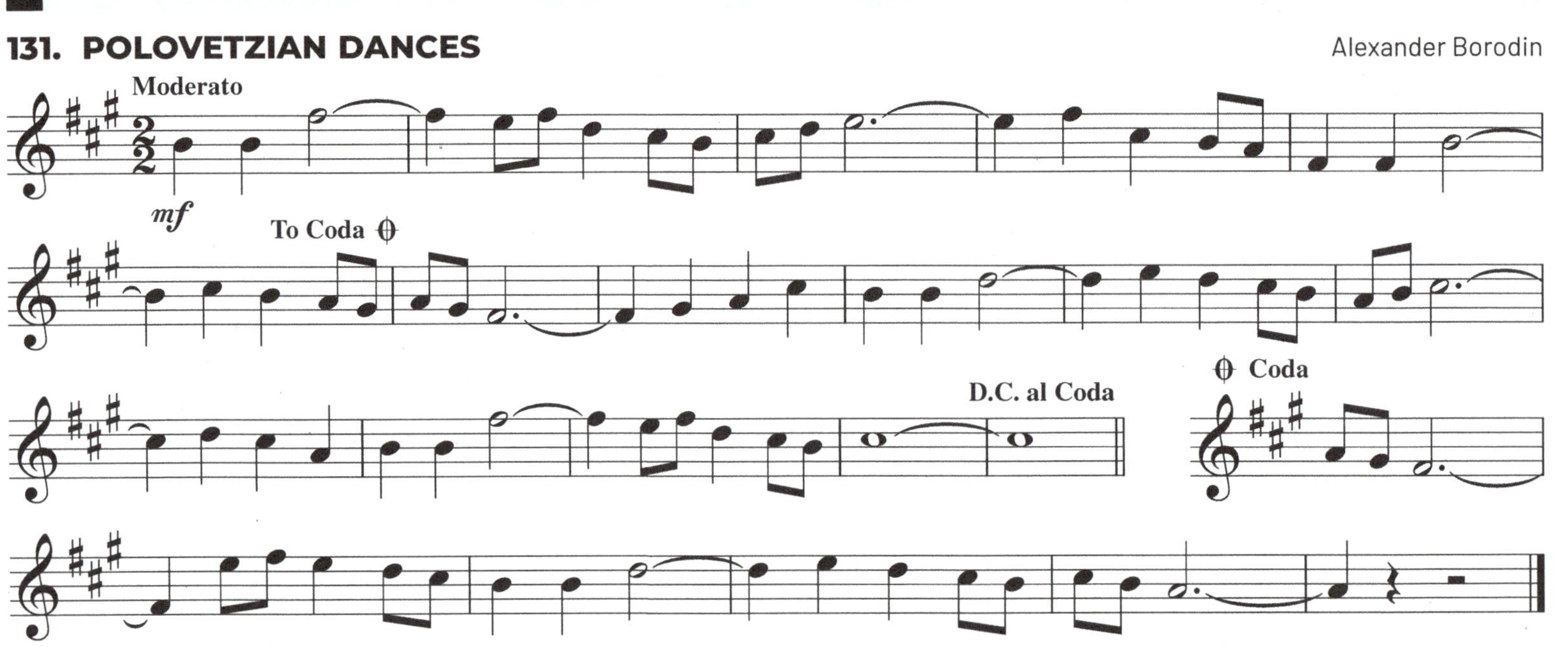

Looking for some more fun music to play?
See the inside front cover for instructions on accessing recent popular Bonus Songs.

E MAJOR (Concert D Major)

132. SCALE AND ARPEGGIO *Practice both upper and lower octaves.*

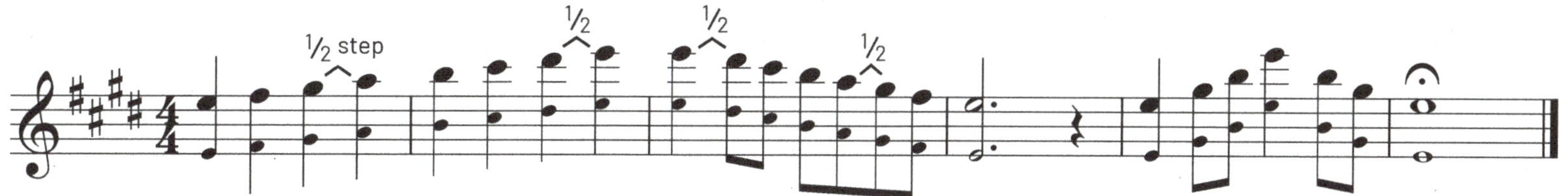

133. EXERCISE IN THIRDS

134. ARPEGGIO STUDY

135. TWO-PART ETUDE

136. CHORALE

C♯ MINOR (Concert B Minor)

137. NATURAL MINOR

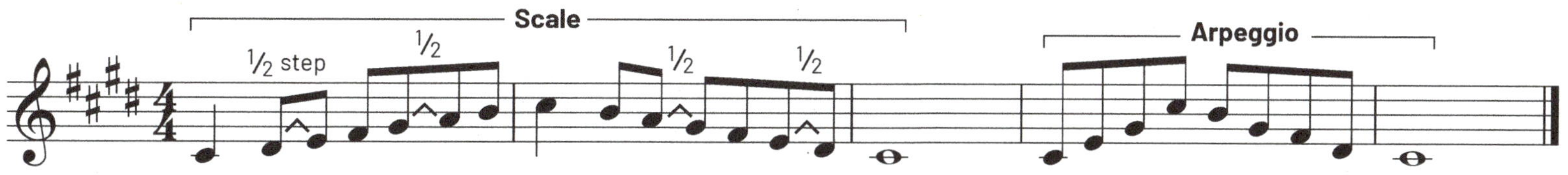

138. HARMONIC MINOR

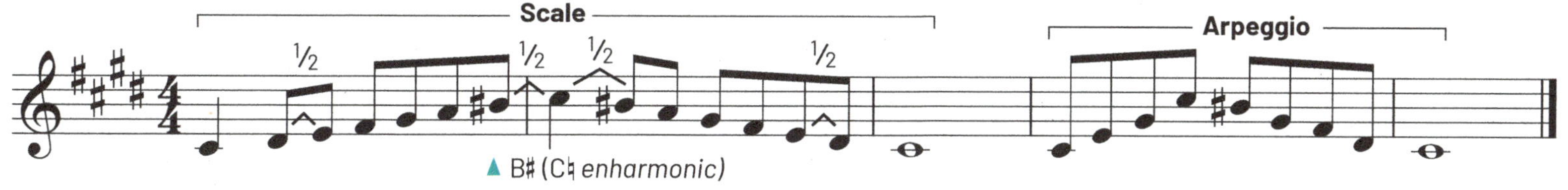

HISTORY

Latin American music combines the folk music from South and Central America, the Caribbean Islands, American Indian, Spanish, and Portuguese cultures. Melodies are often accompanied by drums, maracas, and claves. Latin American music continues to influence jazz, classical, and popular styles of music. *Cielito Lindo* is a Latin American love song.

139. CIELITO LINDO

C. Fernandez

Allegro

HISTORY

Tchaikovsky, along with Wagner, Brahms, Mendelssohn, and Chopin, helped define the musical era known as the **Romantic Period (1825–1900)**. The "symphonic tone poem" from this period continues to be one of the most popular musical forms performed by orchestras and bands today.

140. WALTZ IN FIVE (from SYMPHONY NO. 6)

Peter I. Tchaikovsky

141. THE YOUNG CHEVALIER

Scottish

A♭ MAJOR (Concert G♭ Major)

142. SCALE AND ARPEGGIO

143. EXERCISE IN THIRDS

144. ARPEGGIO STUDY

145. TWO-PART ETUDE

146. CHORALE

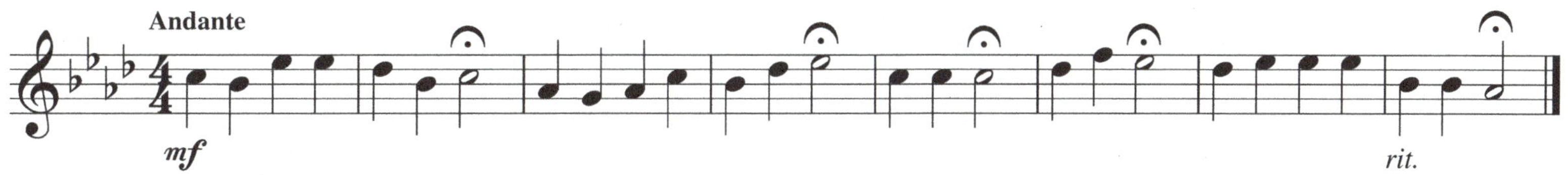

F MINOR (Concert E♭ Minor)

147. NATURAL MINOR

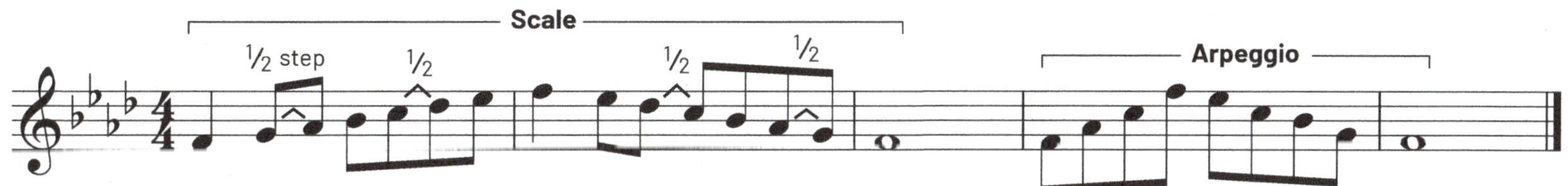

148. HARMONIC MINOR

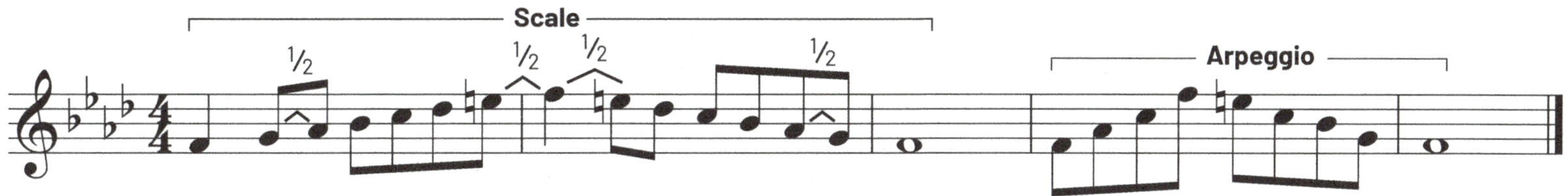

INDIVIDUAL STUDY – Tenor Saxophone

INDIVIDUAL STUDY – Tenor Saxophone

153. EXERCISE IN 12/8

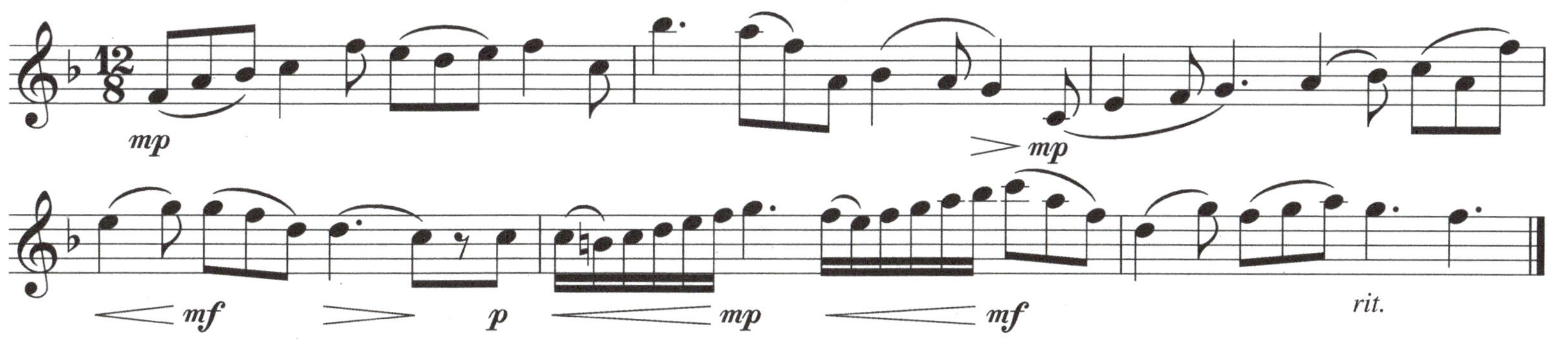

154. CHROMATIC CHALLENGE

155. LEGATO STUDY

156. CONCERT C MINOR STUDY

157. STACCATO ETUDE

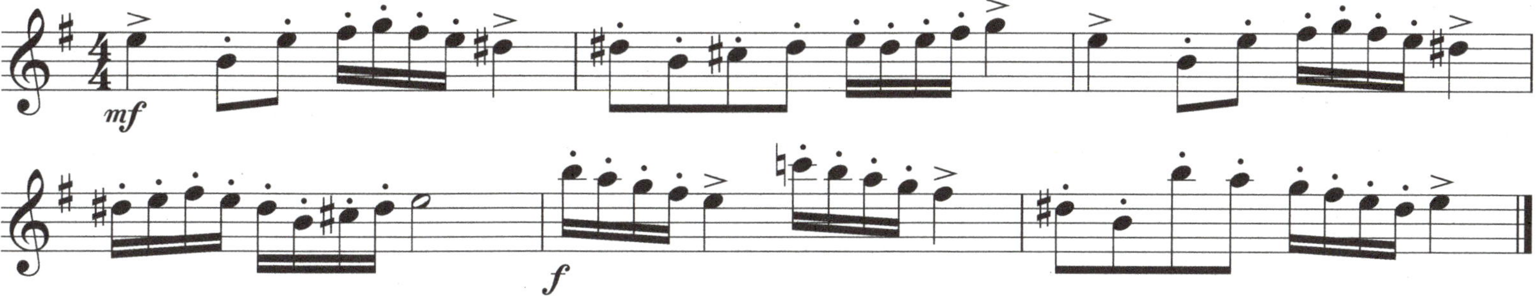

READING SKILL BUILDERS

158. READING SKILL BUILDER NO. 1

mf

159. READING SKILL BUILDER NO. 2

mf *f* *mf* *f*

160. READING SKILL BUILDER NO. 3

f marcato

mf legato 3 3 *f marcato* 3

161. READING SKILL BUILDER NO. 4

162. READING SKILL BUILDER NO. 5

READING SKILL BUILDERS

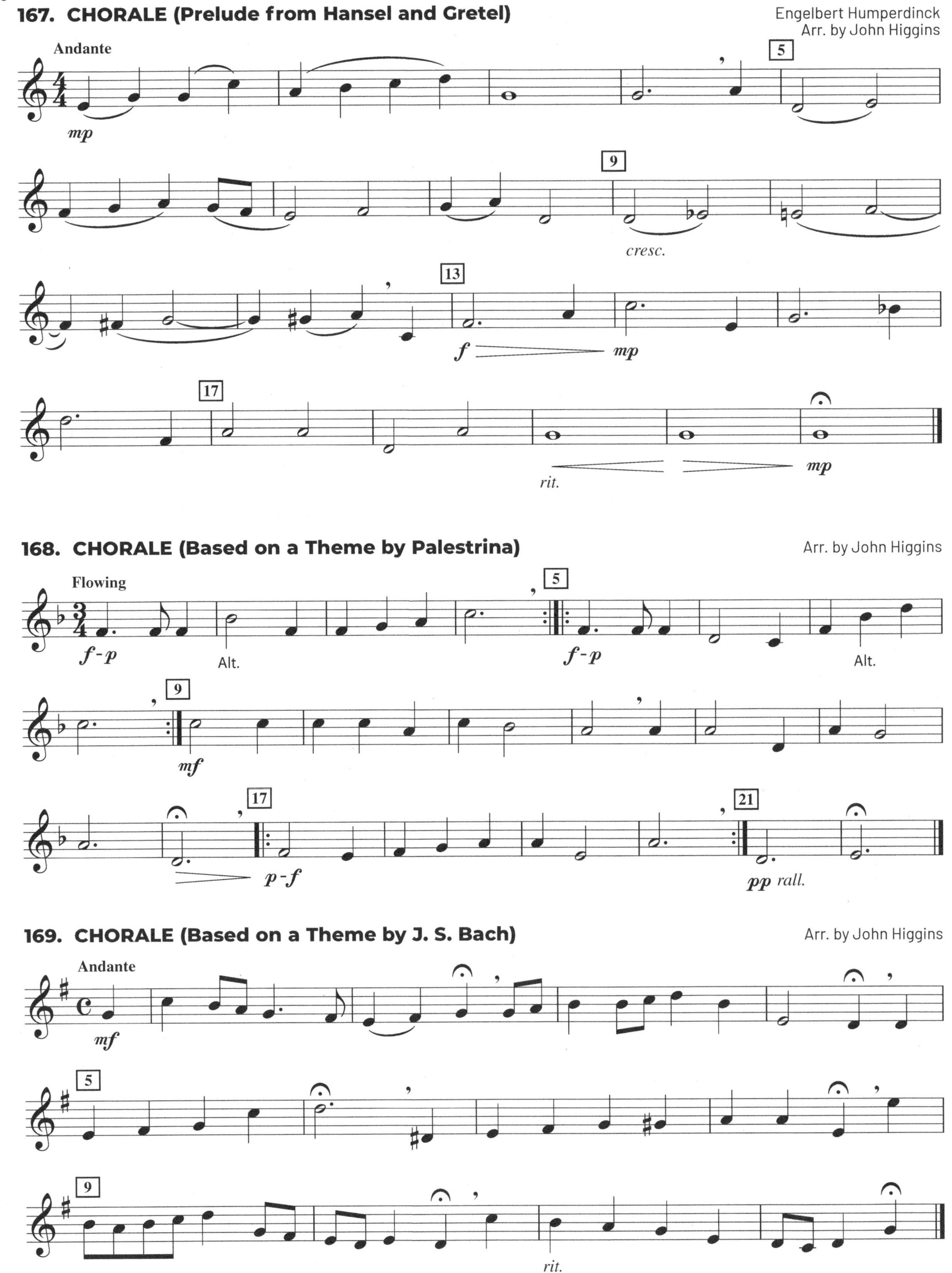
167. CHORALE (Prelude from Hansel and Gretel)
Engelbert Humperdinck
Arr. by John Higgins
Andante
mp
5
9
cresc.
13
f
mp
17
rit.
mp
168. CHORALE (Based on a Theme by Palestrina)
Arr. by John Higgins
Flowing
f-p
Alt.
5
f-p
Alt.
9
mf
17
p-f
21
pp rall.
169. CHORALE (Based on a Theme by J. S. Bach)
Arr. by John Higgins
Andante
mf
5
9
rit.

170. CHORALE (Based on a Theme by Tchaikovsky)

Arr. by John Higgins

171. CHORALE (Erhalt Uns In Der Wahrheit)

Johann Sebastian Bach
Arr. by John Higgins

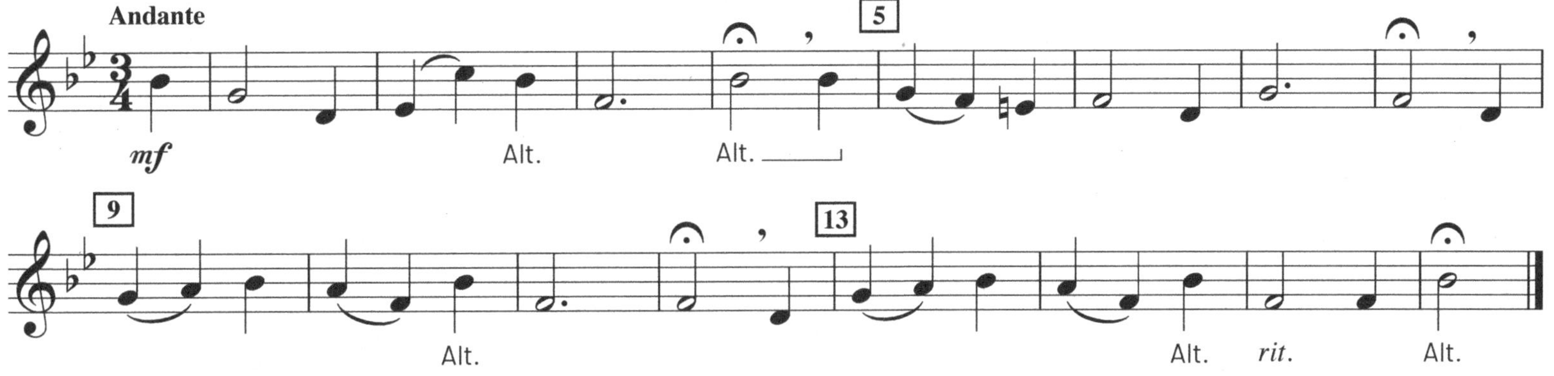

172. CHORALE (Navy Hymn)

John Dykes
Arr. by John Higgins

173. CHORALE (Prelude)

Frederic Chopin
Arr. by John Higgins

RHYTHM STUDIES

RHYTHM STUDIES

57 58 59 60 61 62 63 64

65 66 67 68 69 70 71 72

73 74 75 76 77 78 79 80

81 82 83 84 85 86 87 88

89 90 91 92 93 94

95 96 97 98 99 100

101 102 103 104

105 106 107 108

109 110 111 112

113 114 115 116

THE BASICS OF JAZZ STYLE from Essential Elements for Jazz Ensemble

Accenting "2 and 4"

For most traditional music the important beats in 4/4 time are 1 and 3. In jazz, however, the emphasis is usually on beats 2 and 4. Emphasizing "2 and 4" gives the music a jazz feeling.

174. ACCENTING 2 AND 4

Jazz Articulations

There are four basic articulations in jazz.

Tenuto
(full value)

Staccato
(short, unaccented)

Long Accent
(full value, accented)

Roof Top Accent
(short, accented)

Swing 8th Notes Sound Different Than They Look

In swing, the 2nd 8th note of each beat is actually played like the last third of a triplet, and slightly accented. 8th notes in swing style are usually played *legato*.

175. SWING 8TH NOTES

Quarter Notes

Quarter notes in swing style are usually played detached (*staccato*) with accents on beats 2 and 4.

176. QUARTERS AND 8THS

177. RUNNIN' AROUND

Syncopation in Jazz

When beats are played early (anticipated) or played late (delayed), the music becomes syncopated. Syncopation makes the music sound "jazzy."

178. WHEN THE SAINTS GO MARCHING IN – Without Syncopation

James Black and Katherine Purvis

179. WHEN THE SAINTS GO MARCHING IN – With Syncopation

"Jazzin' Up" the Melody by Adding Rhythms

Adding rhythms to a melody is another easy way to improvise in a jazz style. Start by filling out long notes with repeated 8th and quarter notes. Remember to swing the 8th notes (play *legato* and give the upbeats an accent).

180. "JAZZIN' UP" JINGLE BELLS

J. Pierpont

MAKE UP YOUR OWN (IMPROVISE)

181. LONDON BRIDGE

Complete the melody in your own "jazzed up" way. Use only the notes shown in parentheses. Slashes on the staff indicate when to improvise.

Major Scales

Play major scales as part of your daily practice routine. Play all octaves, keys, and arpeggios at various dynamic levels and tempos. Keep a steady pulse. Try different articulation patterns, such as:

182. C MAJOR (Concert B♭ Major)

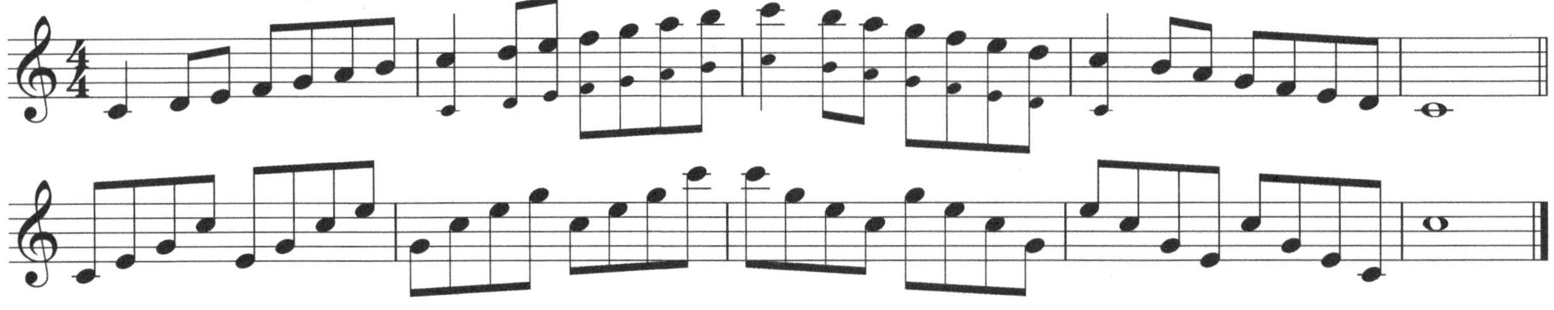

183. F MAJOR (Concert E♭ Major)

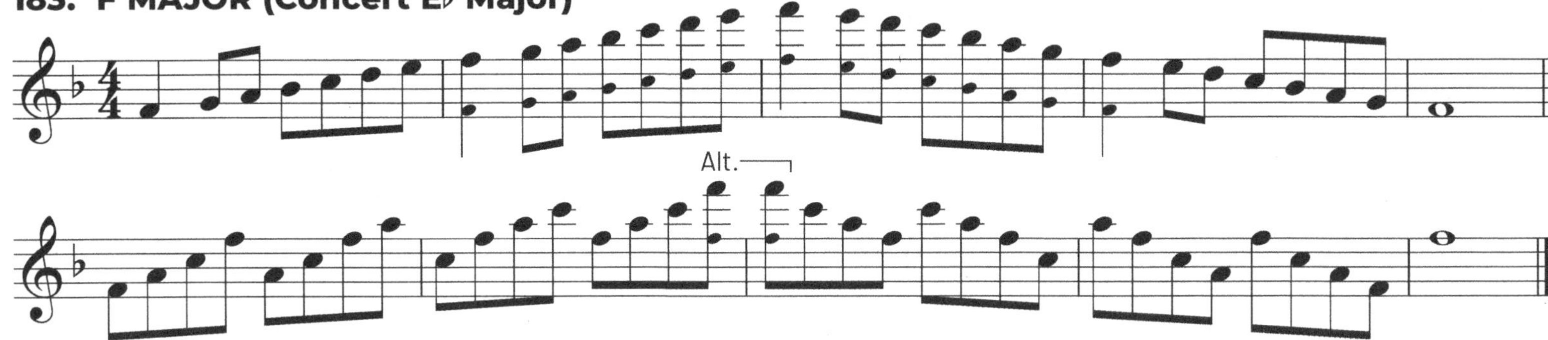

184. G MAJOR (Concert F Major)

185. D MAJOR (Concert C Major)

186. B♭ MAJOR (Concert A♭ Major)

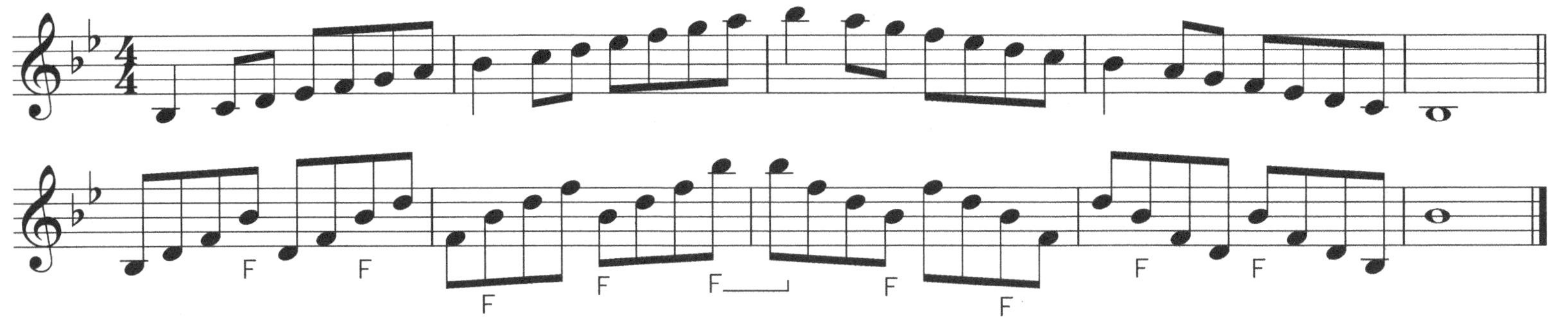

187. E♭ MAJOR (Concert D♭ Major)

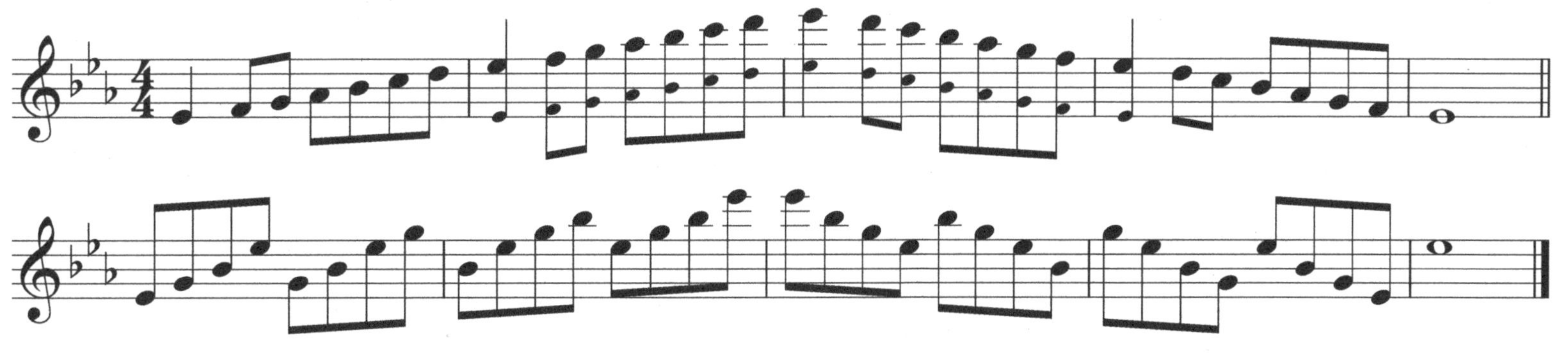

188. A MAJOR (Concert G Major)

189. E MAJOR (Concert D Major)

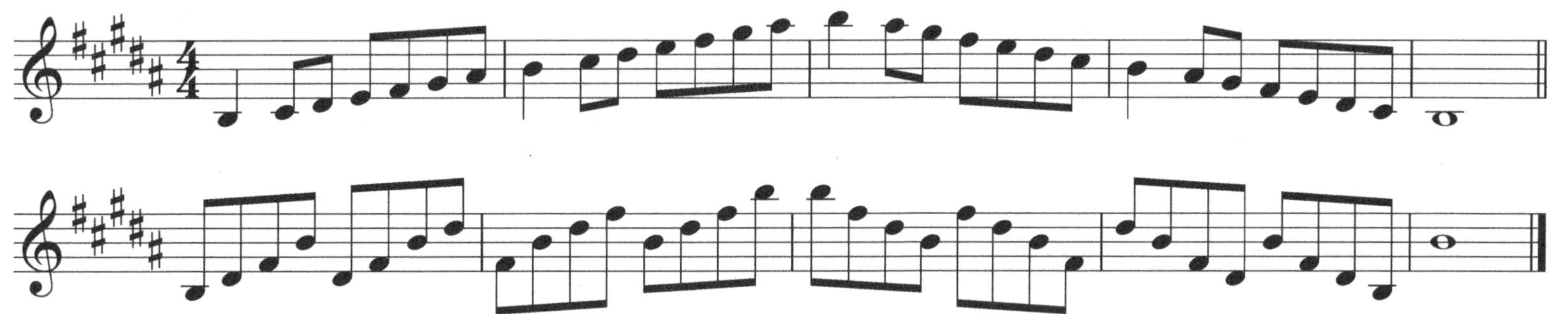

190. B MAJOR (Concert A Major)

191. A♭ MAJOR (Concert G♭ Major)

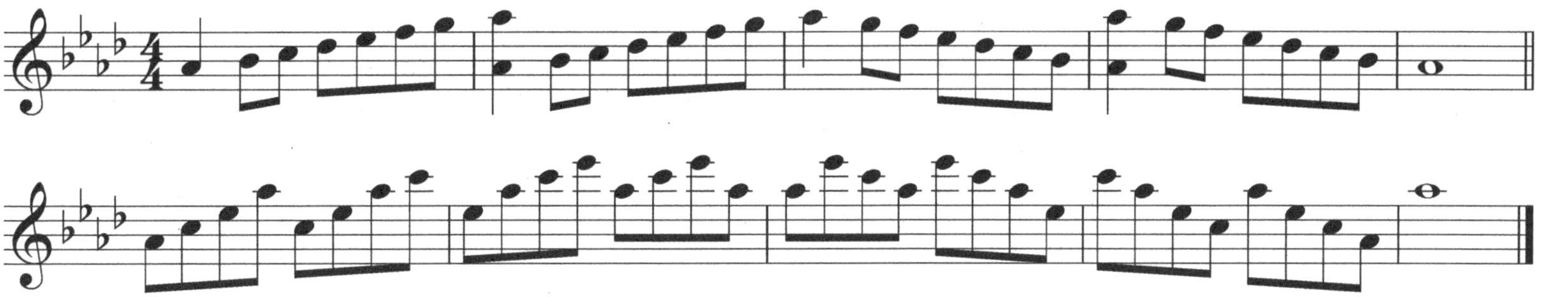

Minor Scales

Play minor scales as part of your daily practice routine. Play all octaves, all three forms, and the arpeggios at various dynamic levels and tempos. Keep a steady pulse. Try different articulation patterns, such as:

192. E MINOR SCALE (Concert D Minor)

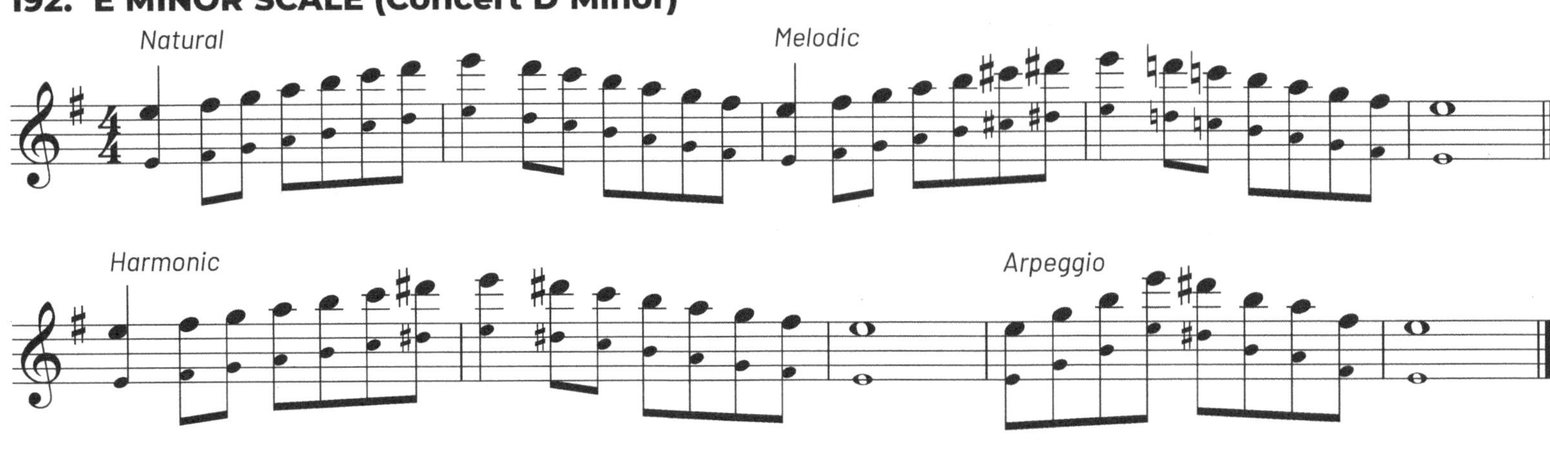

193. A MINOR SCALE (Concert G Minor)

194. D MINOR SCALE (Concert C Minor)

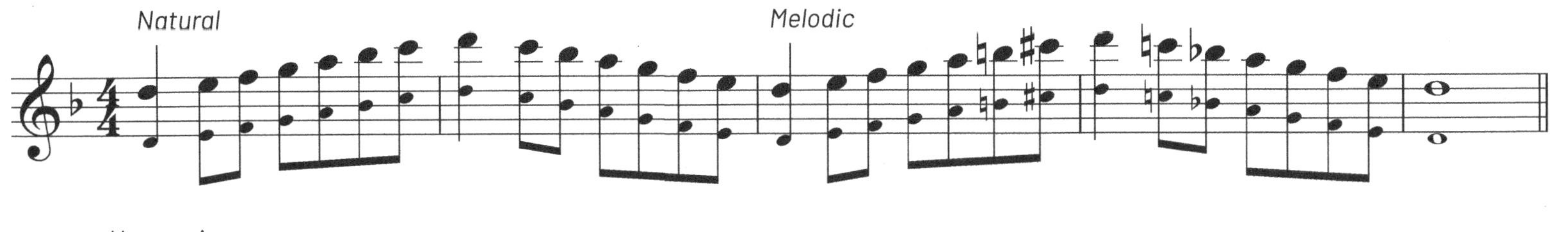

195. G MINOR SCALE (Concert F Minor)

TRILL CHART

B♭ TENOR SAXOPHONE

Here are some common trill fingerings. Trill the **red** key(s).

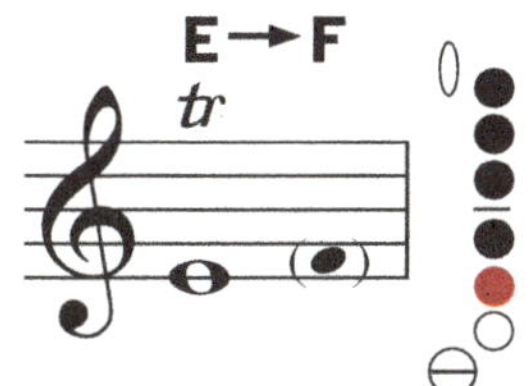

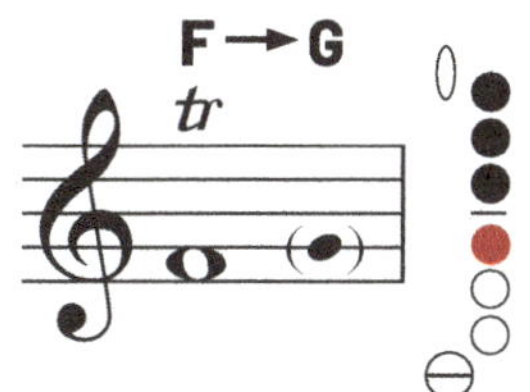

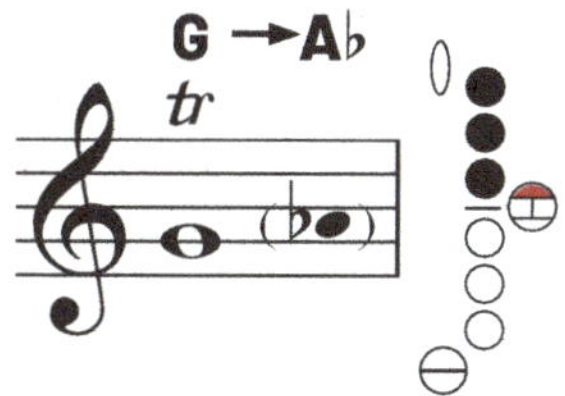

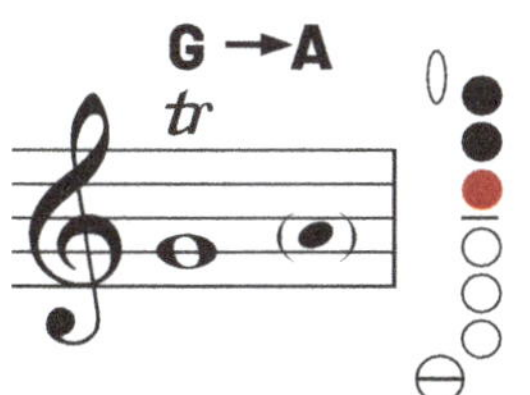

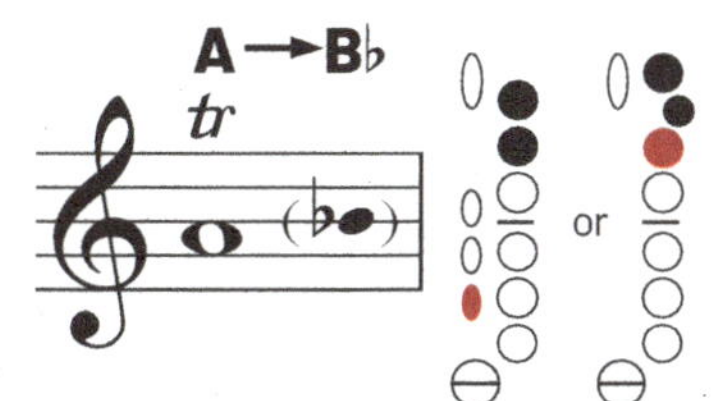

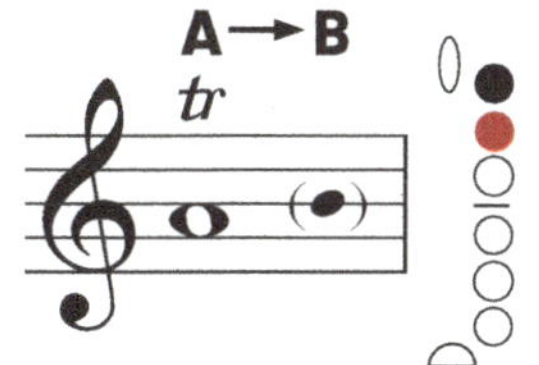

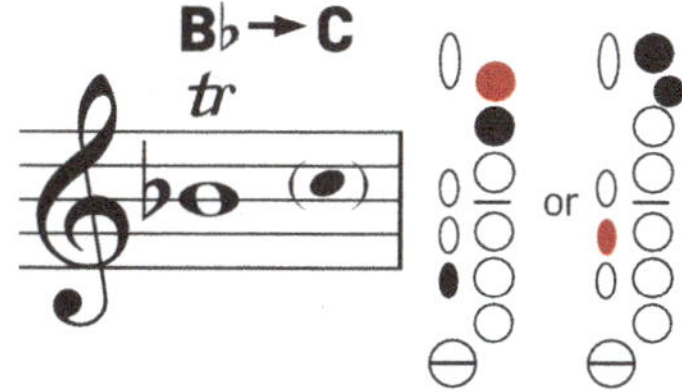

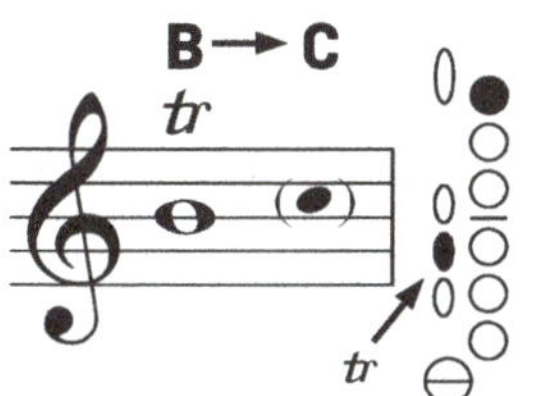

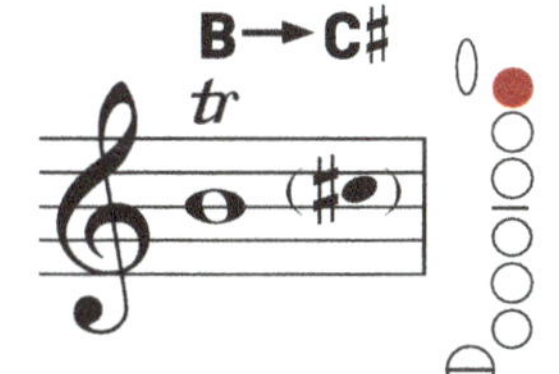

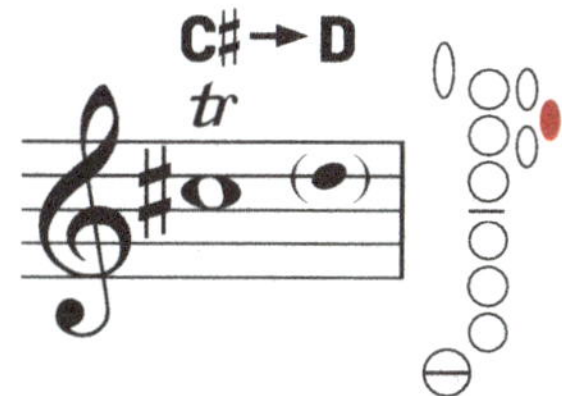

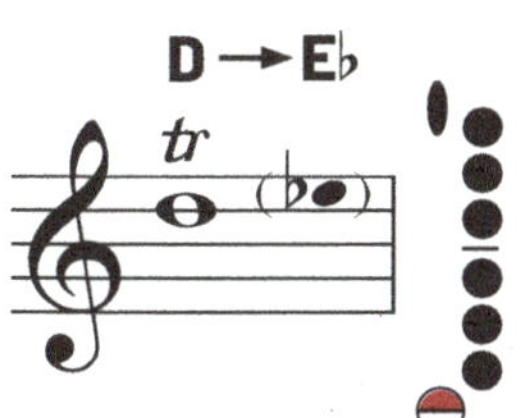

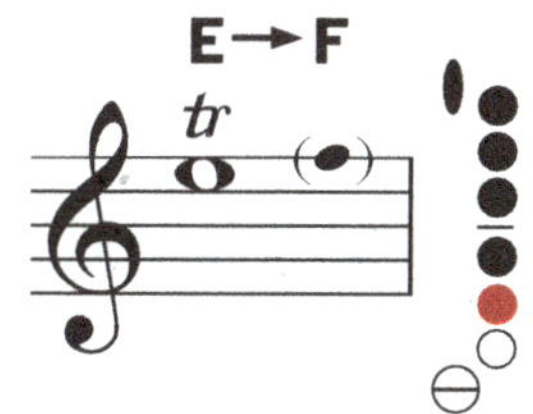

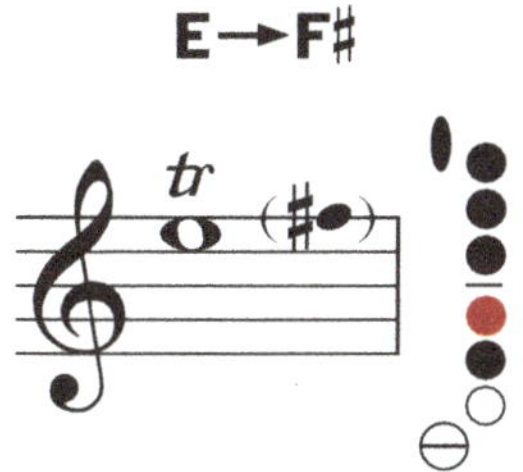

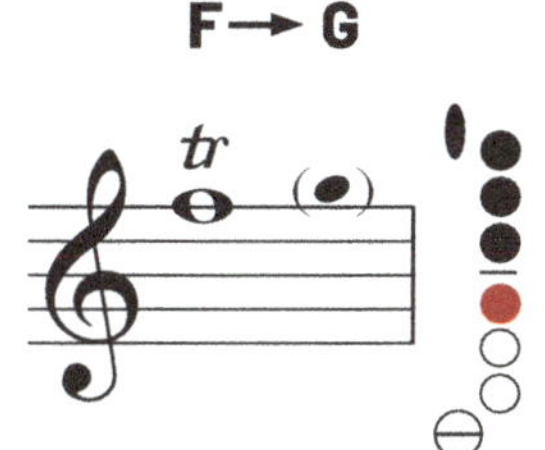

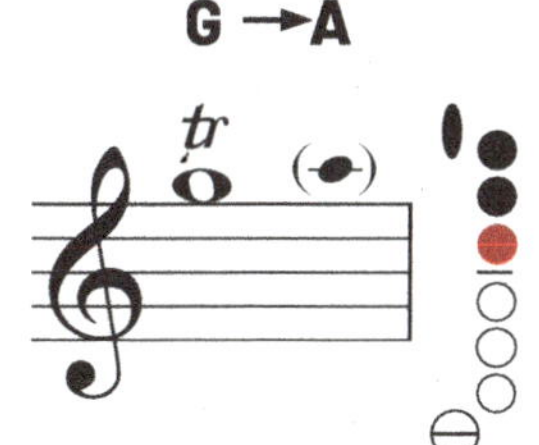

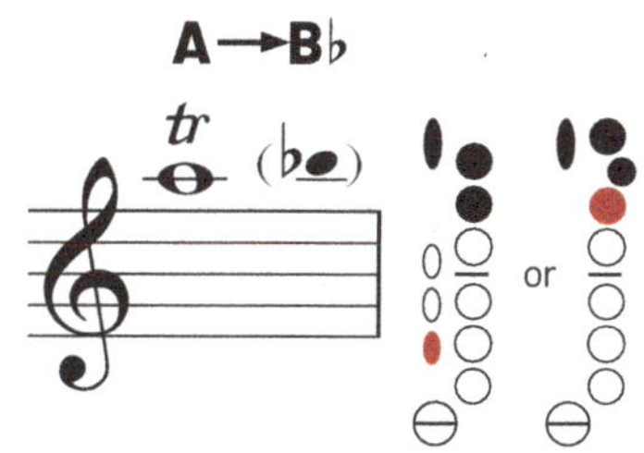

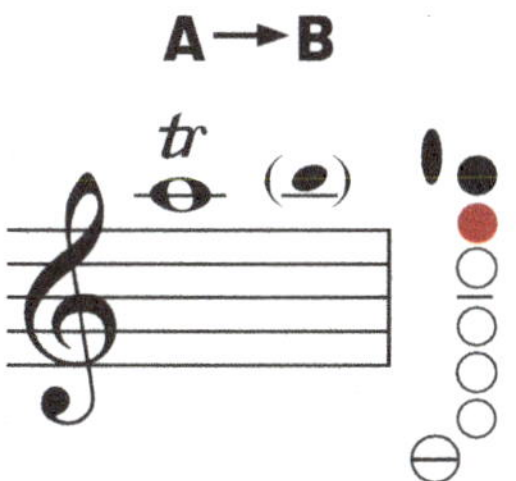

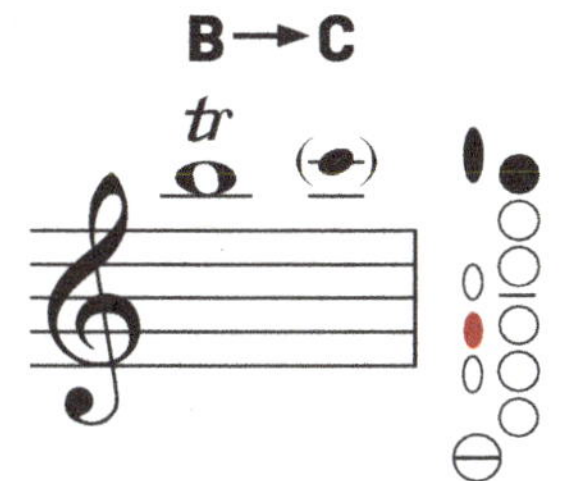

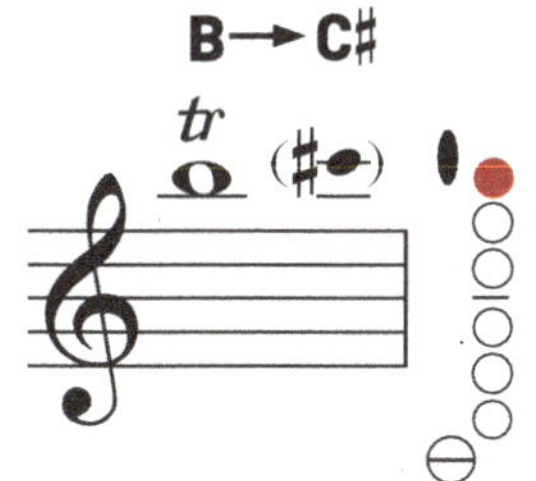

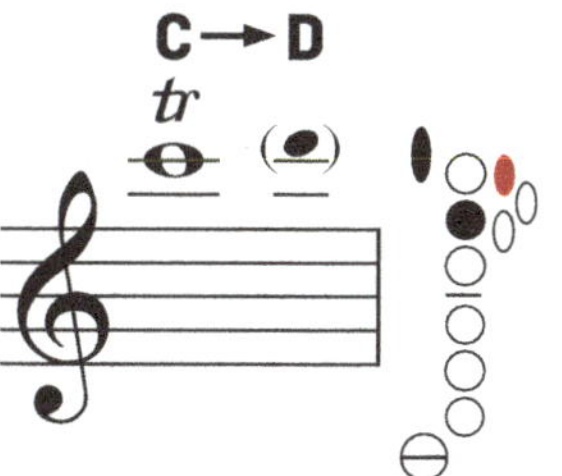

FINGERING CHART

B♭ TENOR SAXOPHONE

Instrument Care Reminders

Before putting your instrument back in its case after playing, do the following:

- Remove the reed, wipe off excess moisture and return it to the reed case.
- Remove the mouthpiece and wipe the inside with a clean cloth. Once a week, wash the mouthpiece with warm tap water. Dry thoroughly.
- Loosen the neck screw and remove the neck. Shake out excess moisture and dry the neck with a neck cleaner.
- Drop the weight of a chamois or cotton swab into the bell. Pull the swab through the body several times. Return the instrument to its case.
- Your case is designed to hold only specific objects. If you try to force anything else into the case, it may damage your instrument.

○ = Open

● = Pressed down

The most common fingering appears first when two fingerings are shown.

Instruments and photos courtesy of Yamaha.

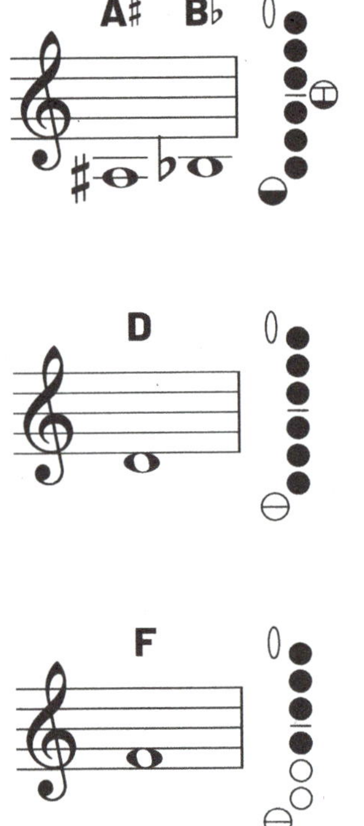

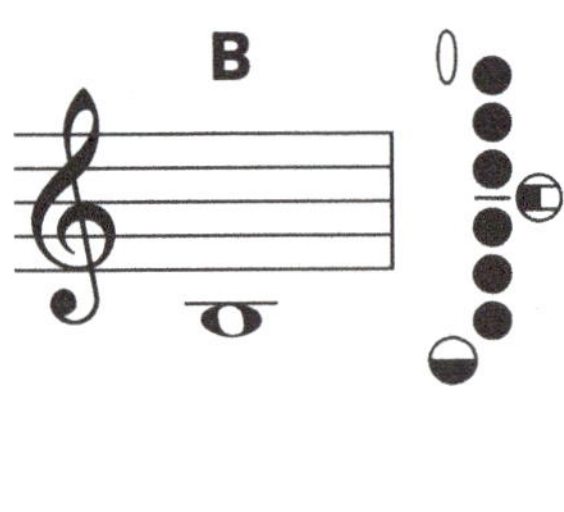

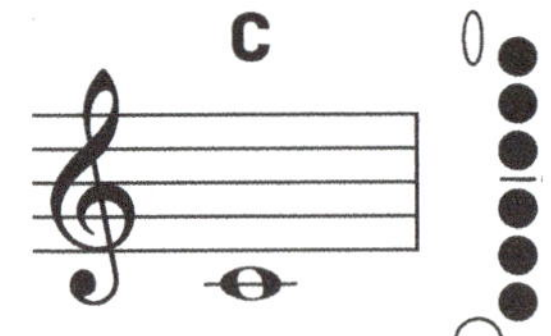

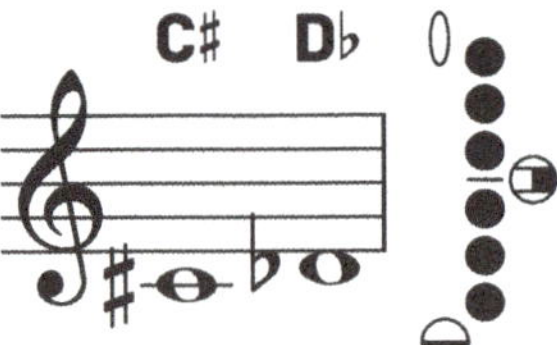

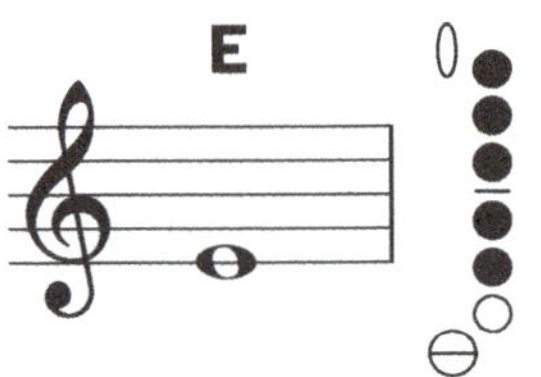

Alt.

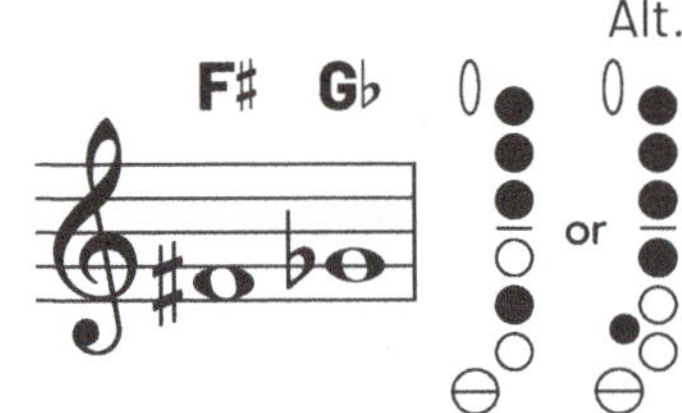

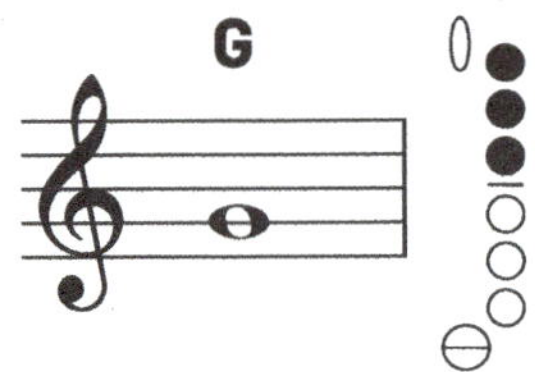

FINGERING CHART

B♭ TENOR SAXOPHONE

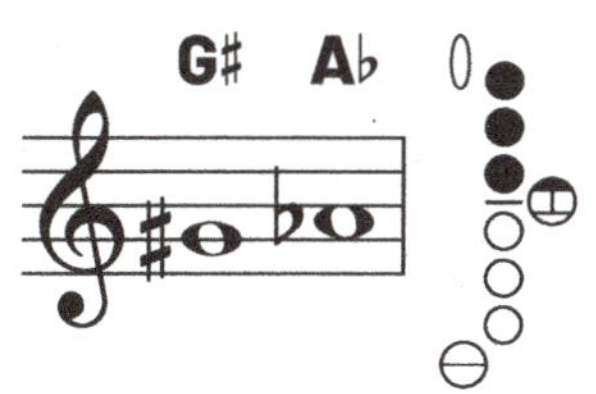

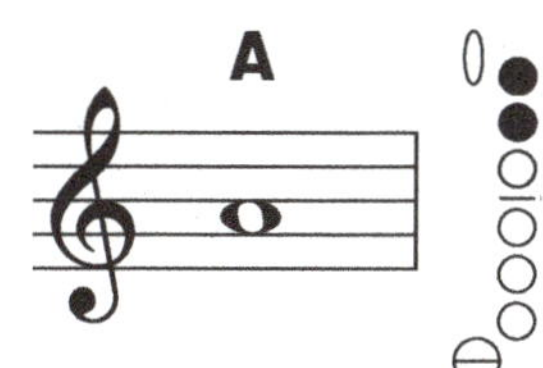

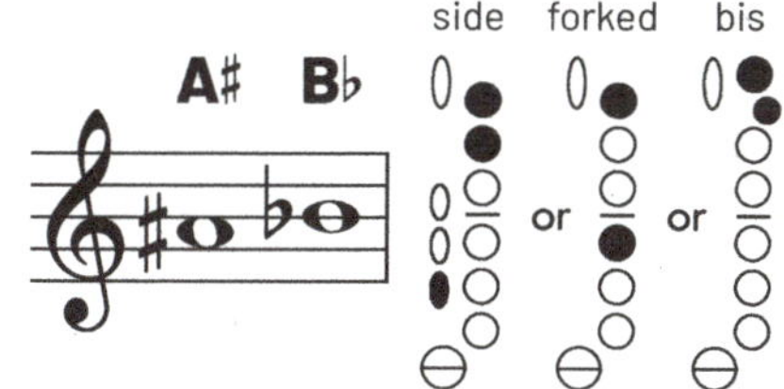

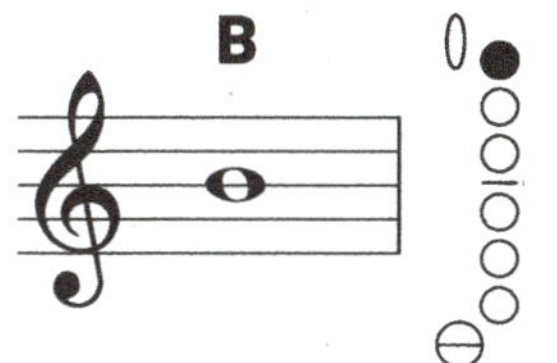

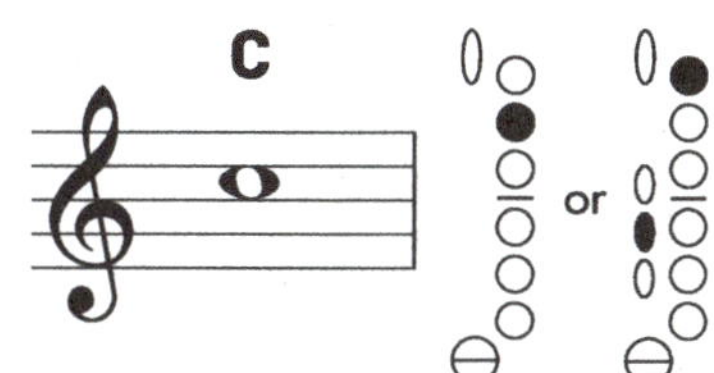

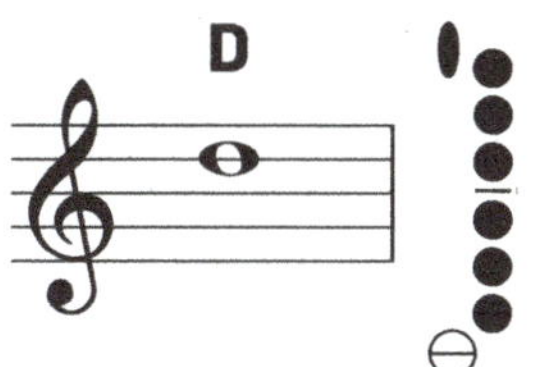

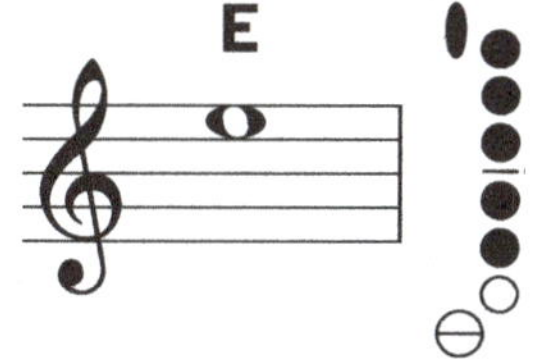

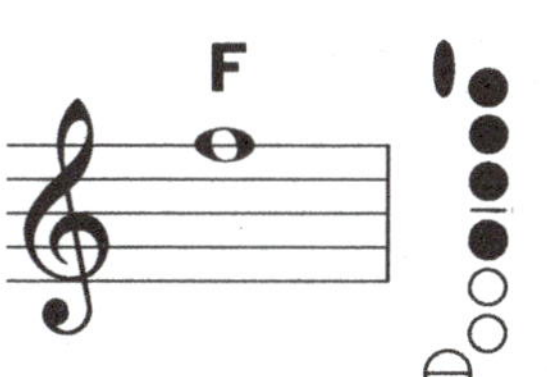

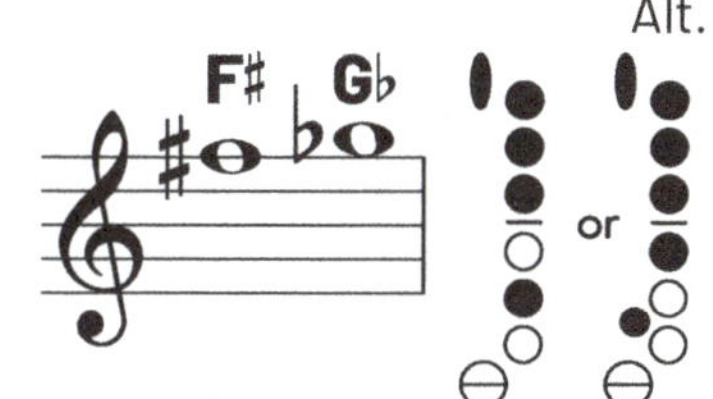

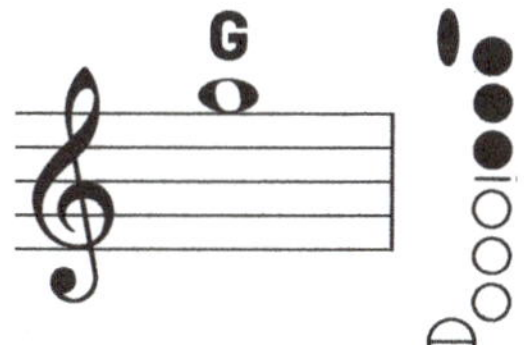

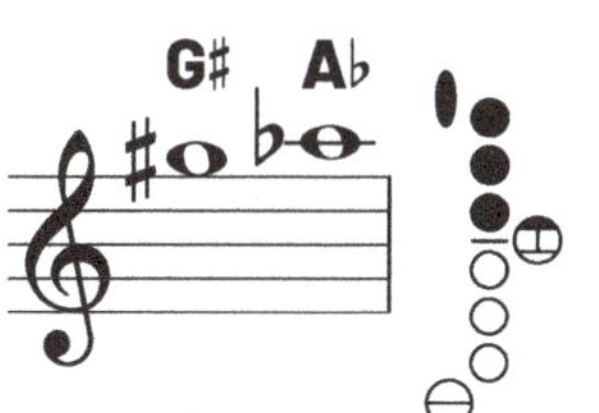

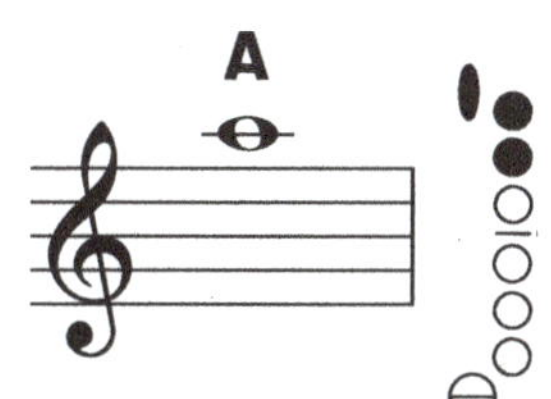

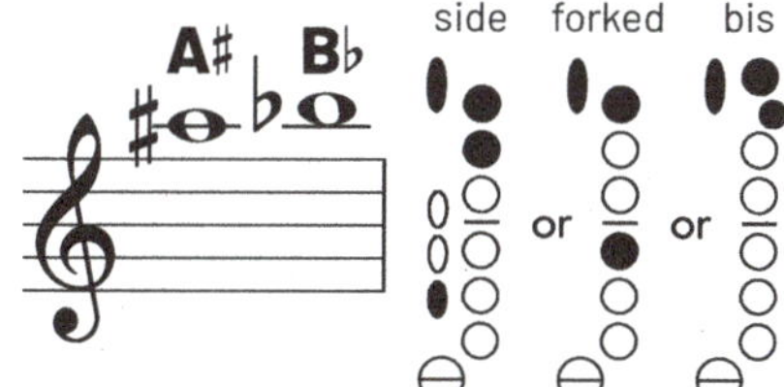

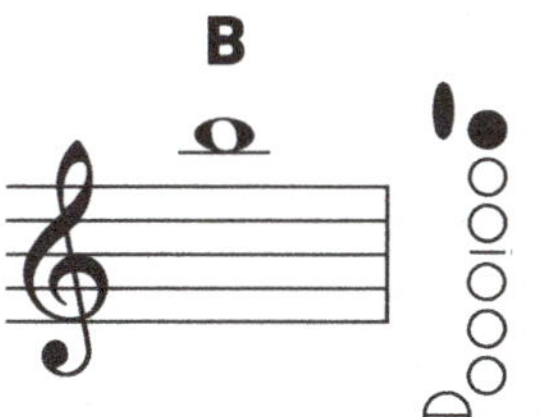

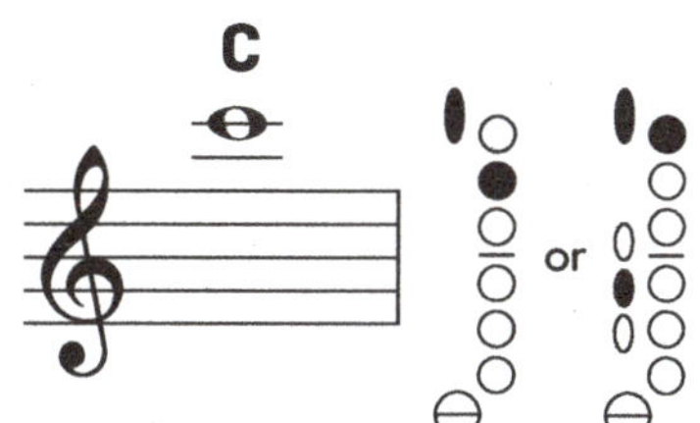

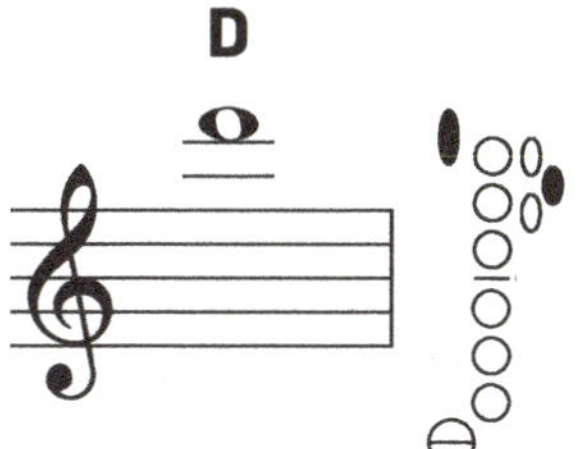

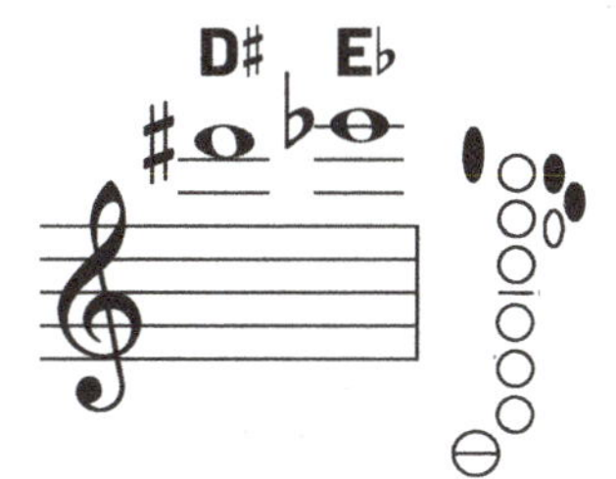

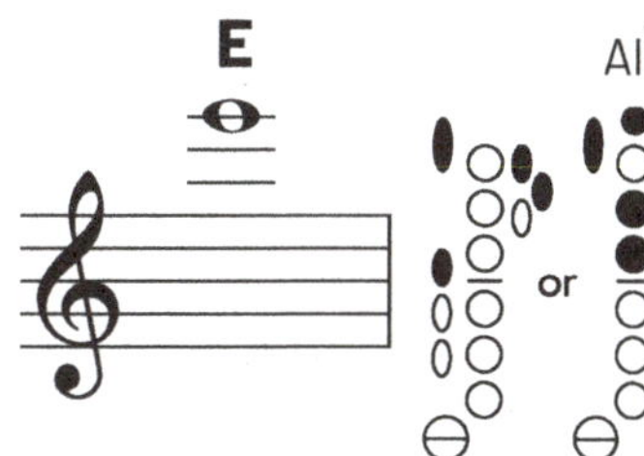

REFERENCE INDEX

Definitions (pg.)

Composers

World Music